The Judo Manual

The Judo Manual

Tony Reay & Geoffrey Hobbs

TIGER BOOKS INTERNATIONAL
LONDON

This edition published in 1993 by
Tiger Books International PLC, Twickenham

Created by The Wordsmiths Company Limited
First published by Barrie & Jenkins Ltd 1979
Reissued by Stanley Paul Ltd 1982

An imprint of Random House UK
20 Vauxhall Bridge Road, London SW1V 2SA

Set in Palatino and designed by Brian Folkard Design

Printed and bound in Italy by New Interlitho spa

A catalogue record for this book is available
from the British Library

ISBN 1-85501-360-6

The creators and publishers wish to acknowledge
David Finch, Bob Willingham and the Budokwai
for permission to reproduce their photographs,
and Sixpenny Studios for the diagrams.

The authors: Tony Reay (left) and
Geoffrey Hobbs, at a judo competition at
Crystal Palace, London.

contents

Forewords — Preface — Darrell Sweany

Charles S Palmer

As a modern Olympic sport judo is practised and competitions take place in over 100 of the countries which are in membership of the International Judo Federation. In Britain alone there are now over 1,000 judo clubs and in Europe judo figures among the top ten leading sports in many countries. In most of these countries judo is now accepted as a part of the schools curricula. Education authorities have found it to be an ideal indoor activity for young people. Judo has a special 'social' value in that more people take part in the sport than merely watching it. Services and police forces have found for many years that judo provides a good basis for physical development along with the significant in-built self-discipline so necessary for service life.

People practice judo for many different reasons. Some consider judo to be an 'art form', developed over the centuries and steeped in tradition. To such people judo is almost a religion and a way of life. They study meticulously and spend many hours of the week perfecting their skills and trying to improve their skill range. They are prepared to go on to the end of their lives striving to develop and perfect those skills, such is the absorbing interest of judo for them. At the opposite end of the scale there are people who find judo to be a reasonable means of keeping fit while at the same time learning something that might be useful.

There are the competitors whose aim is to achieve their goals by way of grades, championships and competitions. There are people who recognise in judo a certain value in the area of self-defence. Whatever the reasons for people wanting to do judo there has to be proper tuition, and together with such tuition the reading of judo books can be of immense value.

What has been needed in recent years has been an up-to-date book which between its covers, contains all the aspects of judo. One which encompasses all the differing readers, with differing interests; one which they can read and have available to use for reference. A book that is useful not just to the competitor, not just to the beginner, not just to the instructor — but one that is prepared and presented in such a way that it has some value to all, a manual which deals with the wide range of judo for all levels of interest. Such a book should be presented in such a way as to help the uninitiated to understand what judo is really all about. This book, 'The Judo Manual', goes a long way towards doing just that.

Both of the co-authors of this book are members of the British Judo Association. One of them, Geoffrey Hobbs, is still competing at our national events and his youthful enthusiasm for judo illuminates its pages. The other author, Tony Reay, commenced judo twenty-three years ago at the famous Budokwai where I was then a senior instructor. Tony then followed the course taken by many of us and dedicated all his free time to judo. Following in the footsteps of those who had pioneered the 'pilgrimage' East, he studied for almost four years in Japan with the Tokyo Police and at Tokyo University. Tony was competing before judo had any weight categories and his 63 kilos and five feet four inches obliged him to train and study much harder than most in order to acquire the skill and technique which was so necessary to enable him to survive an international contest career — one in which he never knew from one contest to the next whether his opponent would be his own weight and size or 126 kilos and six feet four inches! After an impressive contest career he became a full-time judo instructor and eventually Manager of The Budokwai. Having founded a number of local judo clubs, Tony Reay assisted with area administration and eventually became a senior executive of the British Judo Association. As a judo instructor he was involved with all levels of competition and has been described by a leading sportswriter and judo correspondent as being one of those rare people with the ability to teach at all levels – from beginner to international standard.

Charles S Palmer OBE 7th Dan
President of the British Judo Association
President of the International Judo Federation

Phil Porter

We are often used to thinking of sport, and success in sport, in terms of the output of a government machine of scientists, doctors, and coaches who cold bloodedly manufacture champions for the glory of the state. But that whole system is foreign to the social structure of both Great Britain and the United States. We may have many personal reasons for winning, but we usually do it on our own, or with the help of educational or sports organizations rather than government functionaries. You can imagine a Cuban athlete saying, "I did it for our glorious leader Fidel", but you can't imagine Keith Remfry announcing that he did it all for James Callaghan or Bruce Jenner declaring that it was all for Gerald Ford.

I mention these ideas to reveal a viewpoint. Judo can be measured in many ways other than by production of medalists. In fact, we do ourselves a dangerous misservice if we think in those terms only. Judo can also be measured by the happy young people it produces, or by the thinkers who begin their philosophical approach to life under its charm, or in terms of physical education.

In reading the manuscript of 'The Judo Manual', there is much with which to be pleased. I was especially impressed with the illustrations. They are done with verve and dynamic movement. The movement is fluid and controlled, the style is classic. It is really difficult to see how better action photos and drawings could be provided without actual film – with all the limitations in expense, study difficulty and production which film entails. Books are the best teachers of judo off the mat, hence their enduring acceptance over all other media, but when a book approaches film with fluidity of movement and extremely pertinent illustrations, one has a worthwhile product indeed. This is what the student will find in 'The Judo Manual'.

Beyond the strictly technical content of 'The Judo Manual', parts 5 and 6 are of extreme interest to judoists. There is not a single book published on judo in the United States, including two of my own which are judo "best sellers", which has a complete section on training and fitness as is found in 'The Judo Manual' This part alone, composed of six excellent chapters, makes the book outstanding in its field. It is simply impossible to find solid information on diet and training in judo books. 'The Judo Manual' is the first to get this information in print.

Part 5, with its seven solid chapters on contest judo, is another part of 'The Judo Manual' which is irreplaceable at present. A student or advanced player can sit down with this book and study repeatedly, gaining something new each time.

Tony Reay is an old friend of mine from Japan days. He has run the course of contributions to Judo, including a stint as General Secretary of the BJA. I am honored indeed to have been asked to write a foreword for 'The Judo Manual' I recommend it most highly to the judo community in both Britain and the United States.

Philip S. Porter, is a 6th degree (Dan) Black Belt, is a past Chairman of the National AAU—US Judo Committee; a past Chairman of the US Olympic Judo Committee; a former Chairman of the US National Coaching Staff and Technical Director of the Pan — American Judo Union; and has travelled the US with his 'Kodokan on Wheels' judo clinics.

A PROFILE OF DARRELL SWEANY—Consultant Editor

Darrell Sweany has been involved with judo and other martial arts in the United States since 1962. He has served as the Executive Director and General Manager of the United States Judo Association, and has been a member of the National Judo, Karate, and Taekwondo Committees of the Amateur Athletic Union of the United States. He has further served as an officer or member for law enforcement and collegiate committees of the United States Karate Association, the National Junior College Athletic Association, and the National Collegiate Athletic Association.

Mr Sweany has a broad and varied background which makes him one of the leading authorities on the historical and technical aspects of judo and other martial arts in the United States. He is a graduate of the prestigious Pine Crest School, Florida, holds a Bachelor of Business Administration and a Master of Public Administration from Florida Atlantic University, and is further graded as a third degree (*dan*) black belt in judo, karate, and jiujitsu.

Mr Sweany's travels have taken him to forty-five states within the United States, and to more than sixty-five nations throughout Europe, Asia, Africa, and North America. He has trained at many famous institutions from the Kodokan in Tokyo, Japan, to the Anton Geesink Sportschool in Utrecht, Netherlands. Mr Sweany has also served as Managing Editor of **American Judo** and **USJA Coach,** two of the finest judo publications in the world.

Darrell Sweany has experienced all roles of judo and martial arts – a competitor, a coach, and an administrator. The Gold Coast Judo Association and Gold Coast Karate Association, one of the best dojo in the United States which is located in Fort Lauderdale, Florida, was founded by Darrell Sweany. He has also taught college credit courses at Broward Community College in the area of unarmed defense for both law enforcement officers and civilians.

PREFACE—Darrell Sweany

Being asked to be consultant editor of a judo book is not a task to be taken lightly. With so many books about judo in print at this time, surely everything to be said about judo has already been said. After reading **The Judo Manual** by Tony Reay and Geoffrey Hobbs, my attitude has changed.

The Judo Manual brings about for the first time in print many ideas and concepts which previously have only been passed on from instructor to student by word of mouth. The reasons for doing many of the training aspects of judo are explained in this well written book. Many times exercises are given with no reason for their existence other than, "that is the way it is done." The authors give a refreshing approach to many of the aspects of judo that are taken for granted. Furthermore, they have discussed many new areas of health, diet, and training that have never been explored in a judo book before.

The Judo Manual is the most totally encompassing book in print today; it thoroughly covers the many and diverse subjects of modern judo. If the topics were arranged in alphabetical order **The Judo Manual** would represent an encyclopedia of modern judo. Any complete judo library should not be without a copy of Tony Reay's and Geoffrey Hobbs' **The Judo Manual.** The context is of significant value to both the beginner and the lifetime judo player. It is truly an intellectuals' guide to judo.

On the following pages, I have made comments which contrast judo in the United States with that of the United Kingdom. Currently, many coaches in the United States feel that judo has been diminished by the current use of IJF rules in the United States. It is my recommendation that American coaches and competitive aspirants carefully read the items where British champions have commented on their favorite techniques. It is obvious that British judo champions are thinking about ippon score in contest, rather than attaining koka and stalling for time.

Judo is a fascinating Olympic sport. More than that, it is an art form. It is now practised in almost every country of the world. Since it is not part of the Western heritage, its subtleties are not readily understood by people unfamiliar with its original cultural setting. A major aim of this book has been to impart the background information necessary for a proper understanding of this aspect of the sport. Perhaps you are uncertain about judo and want to learn something about it; or you may already have started and are anxious to raise your level of skill. In either case this book will pave the way for you during the formative stages of your judo career. Step by step, information which it has taken others years to assimilate is set down in a way which we sincerely hope will go a long way towards the improvement of your judo.

Many fine books have been published on judo in recent years and inevitably there has been some degree of overlap between them. It would be misleading to pretend that nothing in the text of this book can be found anywhere else. There is, nevertheless, a large gap between the elementary books and those for the advanced player. Traditionally the judo enthusiast has had to bridge that gap the hard way, by bitter experience and enquiry. We hope that the information necessary to close that gap now appears in the following pages. It means nothing to a novice to be told about the importance of *renrakuwaza* (combination techniques) in contest; likewise nobody holding a 1st *kyu* grade (senior student) needs to be told about, for instance, the system of grades used in judo. The inescapable fact is, however, that everyone needs both types of information at some stage in their training. That is why both topics are covered in the appropriate chapters of this book. Obviously it is most convenient to have the relevant material on hand in a single sourcebook.

Beyond merely recording information of importance to a trainee, an attempt has also been made to explain the finer points of skill training. These points are explained in a way which may not yield their full significance to a novice the first time he reads the text concerned. Never mind. Subsequent readings in the light of increased experience should reveal the pith and marrow of the teaching in those selfsame passages.

It is commonly said that people learn by their mistakes. So they do and if people lived forever there would be no harm in allowing them to learn by that route entirely. In reality human life is short, and learning by trial and error wastes it. The benefit of other people's experience is always worth having and to that end we have drawn on knowledge from every quarter in order to put the wisdom of modern judo before the reader. Not every proposition put forward is beyond controversy, but all are tenable as a point of view. Where there is a conflict between the traditional approach to a topic and the modern doctrine the reader should consider both and make up his or her own mind. It is no part of our intention to dictate dogma to the judo public. Freedom of thought and an open mind are infinitely preferable to dogma.

One instance of the way in which judo players project their own personality and viewpoint through judo is via the style adopted when using a particular throwing technique. Though not apparent to the layman, contest men differ tremendously from one another in their manner of execution, and this is something to be encouraged. In time, and with the help of this book, your training might single you out as someone special, someone whom others will identify as a person with a rich understanding of a technique or group of techniques. This book is interspersed with comments made by such people, and their sayings are offered as signposts of individualism in the development of technique.

So that the book may be referred to on particular points of information as necessary, an index has been included. Since an index is best used with an overview of the contents in mind it is desirable for the reader to read the text from beginning to end at some stage. The best time in the case of absolute beginners is probably just after the completion of a beginner's course at a reputable judo club. There is no need to dwell on material which appears to be too advanced; it is enough to scan the pages and form an impression of the subject matter. Reference thereafter should be quite straightforward. Always remember that expertise is not to be had simply by reading; the purpose of reading about judo is to receive ideas which can be put into practice on the mat. If expertise flows from that practice this book will have served its purpose. Until then, keep reading and practising.

Finally, it should be pointed out that publication has come at a time when the organization and structure of judo, particularly in the United Kingdom, has been streamlined to take account of policy decisions in the areas of coaching and promotion. The International Judo Federation rules for the conduct of contests have also undergone changes in recent years. Therefore, although the information contained in the text about weight categories, contests, promotion examinations etc is correct at time of going to press, it is conceivable that (since these are matters subject to continuous review) there may be minor changes from time to time. Your national Judo Association is always happy to advise should any doubt arise.

The word judo translates literally into English as 'gentle art'. Such a translation is misleading, however, because it conjures up the farcical image of a dainty sport in which a flick of the wrist can send a grown man crashing to the ground. In reality the art is an analysis of the skills by which an opponent can be defeated in a struggle at close quarters. *Ju* symbolises a principle of not replying violently to violence and is the antithesis of *Ken* (as in *kendo*: swordsmanship) which denotes the pitting of force against force. Modern judo does not utilize the body as a bludgeon and, despite its original role as a martial art, it is essentially the highest form of wrestling practised anywhere in the world.

The Kodokan Judo institute in Tokyo is the spiritual headquarters of world judo proper. Other organizations promote styles derived from different judo and ju-jutsu *ryu* (training schools), but only Kodokan judo is heir to the concepts codified a century ago by Professor Jigoro Kano and subsequently adopted by the national organizations around the world which now form the International Judo Federation (IJF).

Kano was born in 1860 and flourished during Meiji, the era of dramatic social and political reform which thrust Japan from feudalism into the twentieth century in just forty years. He graduated with a degree in literature from Tokyo Imperial University in 1881 and took a further degree in philosophy the following year. Apart from being the founder of judo, Kano was a leading educationalist and a prominent figure in the Japanese Olympic movement following the revival of the Olympic Games in 1896. As principal of the elite Gakushuin (school for peer's sons), and later as head of education in the Ministry of Education, he used his influence to establish judo as the basis of a revitalized physical education programme in Japan. For services to the nation he was made a peer in 1922. He died returning by sea from a meeting in Cairo of the International Olympic Committee in 1938.

When Kano began his study of ju-jutsu as a young man, the ju-jutsu masters of the martial arts were struggling to earn a living. Although they were willing to teach the skills handed down to them over many generations, there was little interest among people of the succeeding generation. The tidal wave of reform during Meiji characterized everything Western as

Jigoro Kano at the main entrance of The Kodokan, Japan.

desirable, in contrast with the native culture, which was portrayed as old-fashioned.

Additionally, the demise of the *samurai* (warrior) class in Japanese society had reduced the need for instruction which hitherto had sustained the ju-jutsu *ryu.* For many centuries in Japan power had been concentrated in the hands of feudal governors at the expense of a weak central government. Every district governor maintained a private army of *samurai* (from *samarau:* 'to watch over, to guard'), and the right to carry weapons was reserved to them. They became, in consequence, a separate social class; their rigid code of

ethics subsequently blossomed into the vaunted notion, peculiar to Japanese culture, of *bushido* (virtue in warriorhood).

The *samurai* relied principally upon his swordsmanship in combat, but was also expected to train assiduously in bowmanship, horse-riding, ropework, swimming and hand-to-hand fighting. Provincial training schools gave instruction in these arts and until the mid-nineteenth century it was uncommon for anyone outside the *samurai* class to be accepted for training. In 1873 two government edicts brought the existing social structure to an end. Henceforth, *samurai* were forbidden to wear their swords in public and their hereditary pensions were commuted into a lump sum entitlement. In the turmoil which followed the former *samurai* split into two opposing factions; many became policemen able to wear their cherished swords on duty, but many others formed pockets of resistance to the new order in an attempt to restore their class to its former position. Their rebellion was eventually suppressed, but the prestige of the martial arts suffered in the process.

At the age of eighteen Kano studied the ju-jutsu of the Tenshin Shinyo Ryu under Fukudo and Iso, both instructors at the prestigious Komu Sho (central martial arts college; it was superseded by the formation in 1895 of the Butokukai in Kyoto). The Tenshin school was a comparatively modern offshoot of Yoshin *Ryu* which traces its origin back to the late 1600s; its founder had synthesized the best methods practised in his day, an exercise which Kano was to repeat in formulating Kodokan judo.

Following the death of Fukuda, Kano remained briefly with master Iso before finishing his pupilage with master Ilkubo whose method, Kito Ryu, also dated back to the seventeenth century. By 1883, Kano had clarified his analysis of ju-jutsu and related methods to the point at which he felt able to instruct the public through a school of his own. To that end he borrowed a small room at Eishoji temple and opened the first Kodokan for the study of Kano judo.

On a mechanical comparison, judo and ju-jutsu resemble one another. Ju-jutsu was learned as a series of tricks. Joint locks and striking with the hands, feet and elbows were part of the art, and practice had to be carefully controlled. For safety's sake it took the form of stylized attack and defence patterns learned by rote. Although the older schools had progressed to a level at which they possessed a broad repertoire of throws, competitive sparring often resulted in serious injury or even death. No school had reduced its art to a form which embodied the advantages of Kano judo.

The key principle of *Ju*, winning by sleight of body, was adopted but not originated by Kano. Its appreciation is attributed historically to the founder of Yoshin *ryu*, a physician from Nagasaki named Akiyama. Legend has it that he understood the value of yielding in response to an attack when observing trees in a snowstorm. Pine trees stood erect and broke before the storm, but the willow shed snow from its branches by yielding and springing back undamaged.

The exact origin of ju-jutsu and thence of judo is a matter of controversy. Japanese writings refer consistently to a man named Chen Genpin as the source of ju-jutsu in Japan. He is supposed to have fled China after the fall of the Min dynasty and imparted his knowledge to three *ronin* (unretained *samurai*) while lodging with them in the guest quarters at Kokushoji temple in Edo (now Tokyo). Each of the three is held to have developed and improved the system he was taught, thereby founding three schools from

An historic event: the masters of ancient ju-jutsu Ryu gather at Butokukai on 24 July 1906 to formulate modern *kata*. Jigoro Kano is seated at centre front. Kodokan celebrities Nagaoka, Yokoyama, Isogai and Yamashita stand together, the last four on the right.

which all others have multiplied.

Other authorities say that Akiyama learned the art in a rudimentary form in China while studying medicine. The Chinese method was known as Hakuda in Japanese and comprised kicking and striking along with about thirty ways of resuscitating injured opponents. Akiyama is credited with incorporating the willow-tree response into the Chinese system on his return to Japan, so creating a sound basis for the evolution of ju-jutsu.

Kano himself rejected both explanations for a number of reasons. First, ju-jutsu as practised in Japan was unknown in China, where kicking and striking dominated. Second, it is likely that ju-jutsu was given a Chinese parentage in order to endow it with an aura of science and learning. Third, there is sufficient, albeit contradictory, evidence from which to infer that ju-jutsu was known in Japan long before Chen Genpin arrived in 1659. Fourth, given the existence of special wrestling forms in almost every culture, ju-jutsu could easily have evolved spontaneously in a strife-torn Japan policed by professional warriors.

Judo was superior to every method which lacked its own characteristics, but initially that superiority was doubted in some quarters. A number of *machi dojo* (backstreet gymnasiums) decided that the Kodokan was conceited and ought to be put in its place. They visited its premises and caused damage so that if honour were to be satisfied a challenge match would have to be arranged. At such matches the Kodokan was represented by Sakujiro Yokoyama, the outstanding player of his day, and the result was invariably a win for Kano judo.

Similar proof of superiority was required before judo could win acceptance in the provinces. Representatives from the Kodokan travelled to outlying areas and gave lectures on the principles behind the new method. The finale was a contest, with limb locks and striking excluded, between the lecturer and a member of the local training school. A particularly important match took place in 1886 to decide which system of ju-jutsu should be approved for use in military academies, police departments and public schools. Fielding a team of fifteen men, the Kodokan was able to defeat all comers and judo became thereafter a government-approved sport.

Although judo prospered, it

did not remain the expression of a single school of thought. Kano had taken pains to make judo a safe system; in so doing he discarded all ju-jutsu moves he considered dangerous. Nevertheless, some judo teachers preferred to retain more of what he had abandoned and by 1907 their countermove had a significant following in colleges and technical schools. They were aligned with the Kodokan on general principles but operated beneath the umbrella of the Butokukai administration which was loathe to depart from traditional military values. Grades awarded under the authority of Butokukai were recognized by the Kodokan Yudanshakai (*dan* grade society) on application, up to 2nd *dan.* Beyond that the applicant was scrutinized to ensure he was of comparable Kodokan standard before his grade was registered and published in the judo yearbook. For its part the Kodokan maintained a cordial relationship with other schools and was content to proceed by demonstration and example. In the end, post-war controls on judo practice effectively removed all rivals to the Kano school of thought.

The aftermath of the Second World War was a dark era for Japan and things Japanese. As part of Japan's war effort, instructors in the martial arts had been ordered to teach unarmed combat. In retaliation the occupation forces prohibited all practice of the martial arts in schools and public institutions. The ban was not lifted officially until 1951, although there had been a gradual relaxation of the rule in the meantime. Private instruction in judo was tolerated and the police were excepted from the general prohibition. More important, however, the Kodokan was allowed to re-establish itself largely unhindered. Kano had taken a stand against the worst aspects of militarism in pre-war Japan and that, together with new draft

rules which removed the vestiges of judo's martial origin, made Kodokan judo acceptable to the authorities.

In 1949 the occupation authorities indicated that the Yudanshakai of the various schools could be reconstituted as a single democratic organization to fill the vacuum left by the dissolution of the Butokukai. As a result the Japanese Judo Federation was formed under the presidency of Risei Kano, only son of Jigoro Kano, with headquarters at the Kodokan. Administratively, Kodokan judo had become wholly synonymous with the sport of judo, and its first task was to rebuild an interest in judo among a generation deprived of contact with the art.

During the late nineteenth century the rapid westernization of Japan encouraged an influx of foreign professional workers. A number of them discovered an enthusiasm for ju-jutsu and their accomplishments aroused the interest of people in the West. Notable among the early enthusiasts were the prolific writer E J Harrison, who landed at Yokohama in 1897 to become resident correspondent for several newspapers, and Dr Baelz, a German physician attached to Tokyo Imperial University. Ironically Dr Baelz encountered strong opposition when he advised the University that a revival in the martial arts would halt the decline in Japanese physical education. Fortunately, a number of his students were willing to follow the example he set in studying under Totsuka, a contemporary master of Yoshin Ryu.

Serious articles on ju-jutsu began to appear in English after about 1880. Kano was himself co-author of a paper entitled 'Jiu Jutsu, The Old Samurai Art of Fighting Without Weapons' which appeared in the *Transactions of the Asiatic Society of Japan* for 1888/9; three years later the inaugural lecture of the Japan Society of

London dealt with 'Ju Jitsu: The Ancient Art of Self-Defence by Sleight of Body'. Despite being attired in evening dress, the lecturer, Mr Shidachi, demonstrated a few moves on the Society's secretary who was similarly attired. The popular press was nevertheless determined not to be impressed. The British *Saturday Review* assured Mr Shidachi that 'the good old English word "wrestling" translates ("ju jitsu") to perfection'. He was 'mistaken in thinking there is anything new to us, or even very Oriental, in Ju Jitsu', because 'against a third-rate West Country wrestler who was on the watch, it would most assuredly end in the straight throwing of the wrong person.'

In fact, when the time came, there was most assuredly not any straight throwing of the wrong person. With the intention of establishing a ju-jutsu school in England, Mr E W Barton Wright, an engineer who had studied ju-jutsu in Japan, sponsored the visit in 1899 of a team of Japanese experts. The project failed but those of the visitors who stayed took to the stage to earn a living. Best-known among them was Yukio Tani, who toured the music halls offering challengers prepared to wear a small canvas jacket £1 per minute for every minute they lasted beyond five and £50 if they defeated him. The prize money was rarely (if ever) paid, and it soon became necessary to pre-arrange fights so as to give the public their money's worth. So much for third-rate West Country wrestlers!

Barton Wright was a flamboyant figure who never missed a chance to publicize what he branded 'bartitsu', being his own version of ju-jutsu. At an exhibition staged for the Japan Society in 1901 he boasted that he shortly expected the arrival of the best ju-jutsu man of his acquaintance, Sadakazu Uyenishi. Uyenishi also went on the stage during his stay in England but before returning to

Japan in 1911 he had become instructor to the Army Gymnastic Staff HQ at Aldershot, established a respectable ju-jutsu school in Golden Square, London, and published a textbook on his methods in English.

On stage the Japanese showmen performed a number of frivolous tricks which became inseparably linked with ju-jutsu in the public imagination. Uyenishi used to walk forward against the resistance of a pole pressed lengthwise into the hollow below his Adam's apple with all the effort that an adult member of the audience could muster. Similarly, he and other showmen used to escape from beneath a pole pinned across the throat. Three men would press down on each end; two men would stand on the escaper's body; one more would hold each leg. The escape took twenty seconds. For all their showmanship, these men were very capable ju-jutsu players. Their real contribution to the growth of judo outside Japan was made in the books they

published and the instruction they gave.

Tani remained in England after his compatriots had returned home and in 1920 was formally appointed chief instructor to a new club for 'the study of systems developed by the **samurai**': the Budokwai. Neither he nor the club's founder, Gunji Koizumi, could have forseen that they were creating an institution soon to become the most famous judo school outside Japan. Tuition was given in judo, **kendo** (swordsmanship) and other aspects of Japanese culture; Tani continued as instructor until a stroke forced him to retire in 1937. Tragically, the great athlete never practised again and after a long illness died crippled and penniless in 1951.

Koizumi was to European judo what Kano was to world judo. He came to Britain in 1906 by working his passage on a ship from Bombay to Liverpool but within a year he had moved on to the USA to study electrical engineering. Some years after returning to England, Koizumi

decided to open the Budokwai as a cultural centre and social club for the Japanese community in London. His own ju-jutsu teachers were men of the Tenshin Shinyo Ryu but he was a gifted judo player and not at all partisan about the method of instruction at the club. The official opening took place on 26 January 1918 and within four months the membership had grown to forty-four including two Englishmen. The secretary was a man named Steers. He had practised ju-jutsu under Uyenishi in 1904 and had also travelled to the Kodokan for further instruction in 1912 at the age of fifty-five.

From the beginning the Budokwai staged an annual display of judo and associated arts for the benefit of the general public. The first was held at the club's own premises in Lower Grosvenor Place, London, but as the productions became more ambitious successively larger arenas were required in order to accommodate the audience. By 1951 the Royal Albert Hall had become the permanent venue. Judo men travelled long distances to see the shows because they were educative as well as entertaining. Sadly, after the last Royal Albert Hall Black Belt Show held on the 50th anniversary of the club in 1968, the Budokwai committee decided that the club could no longer afford such an annual commitment; the vacuum which was created has never been filled since. The 50th anniversary show lived up to the standard set in previous years; it featured an international club match, demonstrations and displays by instructors and senior grades, with Anton Geesink, the Dutch World and Olympic Champion, presenting a grand finale in a one-against-ten line-up.

The Budokwai educated several generations of judo men at a time when genuine judo clubs were few and far between. For many years it was the only

Yukio Tani demonstrates a self-defence technique on Gunji Koizumi, c. 1920.

authoritative source of Kodokan judo in Europe. The link had been forged by Jigoro Kano during an extended visit to Britain in 1920. Both Koizumi and Tani received Kodokan grades from Kano before he left and from then on a busy import and export operation in judo knowledge was conducted via the Budokwai. A steady stream of Englishmen went to Tokyo for advanced training and films, technical advice and (from time to time) high-grade instructors were made available to the Budokwai. Under Koizumi's influence this expertise reached a wide audience by means of short training courses, demonstrations and the columns of the Budokwai *Quarterly Bulletin,* which had subscribers in every corner of the globe.

Koizumi's vision for the growth of judo on an international basis began to materialize in 1948. On 24 July that year the British Judo Association (BJA) was established as the representative national body; four days later a meeting under the chairmanship of Trevor Leggett, the most senior non-Japanese player in the world, approved the constitution of a European Judo Union (EJU) to represent judo in the continent of Europe. Three years later still, the International Judo Federation (IJF) was created as an inter-continental body with overall control of judo. Koizumi had played a major role in establishing these organizations but as time went by he preferred to make his contribution to judo through the medium of the Budokwai. The club moved to its present premises in 1954 and as its president he inspired the high standards that obtain there still. When finally satisfied in 1965 that his duty to the community had been fully discharged, Koizumi laid down his own life and stepped silently out of judo.

Judo was known elsewhere in the world wherever expatriate Japanese gathered, although it was not practised extensively until after the Second World War. In the United States judo gained an early foothold because of the interest shown by Theodore Roosevelt. As an expression of goodwill Kano sent Yoshiaki Yamashita, a high-ranking member of the Kodokan, to America in 1902 to be his personal instructor. Roosevelt trained regularly, if clumsily, and in due course a room was set aside at the White House for judo purposes. It was thirty-odd years, however, before an American reached *dan* grade in the USA itself.

Large numbers of Japanese immigrants settled in cities along the western seaboard at the turn of the century. Among them were a few high-calibre judo men. Clubs were established for the practice of judo in Seattle in 1903 and Los Angeles in 1915, but for cultural reasons the art was slow to spread beyond these communities. The Second World War was a mixed blessing for American judo in this connection. Japanese-American citizens were uprooted and relocated for the duration of the war; this tended to disperse their culture but regrettably the martial arts came under suspicion as a threat to good order at the relocation centres. *Kendo* was banned completely, and judo was only allowed on a limited basis. As a counter-balancing gain, many servicemen lived in Japan as part of the army of occupation and acquired first-hand experience of judo. On their return home, their expertise gave a tremendous boost to judo.

Australian judo owes much to the efforts of Dr A J Ross. He went to Japan with his parents at the age of nine and took up judo at the Kodokan when he was fourteen. As a *dan* grade he later emigrated to Australia in order to study medicine. The method he used to arouse interest in judo was the same as that employed by Tani in England. He joined a travelling theatre company and used to invite all-comers to fight him as they pleased, while he relied solely on his skill in judo to defeat them. Even though he was a well-built man, it was quite an achievement to remain undefeated throughout the tour. In 1928 he founded the Brisbane Judo Club and the Australian Judo Council; as a 3rd Dan grade he was unarmed combat instructor to the services during the Second World War. Judo reached New Zealand via Australia in 1948 when G Grundy, a 2nd Dan from the Budokwai, opened a club in Auckland.

The most successful newcomer to judo is the USSR. Strictly speaking, a form of judo has been practised in the Soviet Union since about 1930, when Anatoly Kharlampiev and some associates carried out a study of different wrestling systems. They examined judo, Graeco-Roman wrestling, Turkish wrestling and all the different forms peculiar to the Soviet states. In much the same way as judo is a synthesis of ju-jutsu methods, the sport they devised, known as sambo, is a synthesis of the methods they studied. The word 'Sambo' is shorthand for the phrase in Russian which means 'self-defence without weapons'.

In 1938 sambo became the Soviet national sport. The participants wear a tight-fitting jacket over their wrestling costumes and soft leather boots. In order to win outright a competitor must throw his opponent cleanly onto his back while maintaining an upright position himself. Should the thrower fall to the ground, the match continues until one or other of the players secures a groundwork hold or joint lock. Unlike the great majority of non-judo systems, sambo rules permit the wrestler to throw with a footsweep or strong leg action.

Because of the absence of international competition in sambo outside the USSR, the

Russians turned their attention to other possible outlets for the talent they possessed and in 1962 a Soviet judo team comprising sambo men in judo suits collected five medals at the European judo championships. Since then the trend has been for the Russians to dominate in the heavier categories of judo and wrestling, while the Japanese dominate in the lighter categories of the same two sports.

Sambo is a close cousin of judo, but it lacks the same conceptual framework. Strength is viewed differently in the theory of each sport; where theory gives way to the reality of the contest, however, the strength of a sambo wrestler creates problems for heavyweight judo men because there is no upper weight limit in their category. In lower-weight categories, judo men have competed with success against sambo wrestlers in the USSR and it can be seen as an implied compliment that the Russians have stepped up considerably the emphasis on judo during recent years.

CHAPTER 3.   RELEVANCE OF JUDO

The significance of judo is implicit in the answer to a pointed question: why is Devon and Cornwall wrestling not an Olympic sport in its own right? The style dates back to AD 400-500 and has enjoyed a good following in the West of England and Brittany; the wrestlers wear a loose jacket, grip at the collar and sleeve and use throws recognizable as major judo techniques. In short, the resemblance with judo is striking and yet in Olympic terms the sport is a nonentity. The style is merely one branch of wrestling, which in the generic sense of the word covers a multitude of geographically unrelated styles stretching back into prehistory. To be fair, the question posed might have queried why Cumberland and Westmorland, Icelandic Glima or Central Asian Koresh wrestling are not Olympic sports either. All are older than judo; all have something in common with it. In every case the answer is that none of these methods is as comprehensive as Kodokan judo; they lack both its sophisticated repertoire and its emphasis on personal development.

Once it is accepted that sport can ennoble the human animal, the worth of any given sport is its ability to allow free expression of the desired qualities. Wrestling is acknowledged as a character-building pastime. It encourages endeavour, resourcefulness, courage, skill, self-discipline and health. This accounts for its popularity over thousands of years. Of these attributes skill is paramount because there can never be anything noble in crudeness and gratuitous brutality.

In many types of wrestling the skill contest is artificially limited by the rules. Broad objectives such as the breaking of a stance (e.g. arm wrestling or tug of war), the toppling or pinning of an opponent, or the forcing of a submission can be identified, but the curious fact is that regional wrestling styles tend to restrict themselves to one objective to the exclusion of the others. Between systems with the same objective, there is similarity of approach. Each is skilful in its own way, but the scope for cross-fertilization with the skills of dissimilar systems is missing.

Several types of wrestling have been created by deliberate cross-fertilization. Sambo wrestling emerged in the 1930s, International Olympic Freestyle in about 1920, judo in about 1880 and French (i.e. modern) Graeco-Roman in about 1860. All of these forms have comprehensive repertoires and are character-building in the terms defined above. Judo is superior, however, because it embodies more skill, the paramount virtue. Wrestling is attack and counterattack; to that, judo adds the theory of teasing momentum out of movement.

Kano summarized the element of skill in judo as *sei ryoku senyo*: maximum efficiency in the use of mind and body. Maximum efficiency is the hallmark of a skilful throw. Even though it would require brute force to bring about the same result inefficiently, maximum efficiency does not mean that no strength is used in judo. 'Efficiency' simply means that according to the circumstances strength is used in the most useful way; it is an evaluation of purpose, not power.

The problem in judo is to take a man off his feet against his will. In the nature of things, the human body must be carried erect in order to maintain its balance while moving. A man who has lost his balance is liable to fall, and there is always a point at which recovery of balance becomes impossible. Clearly the creation of imbalance in an opponent is the most useful application of the strength available to a judo player. No matter how strong an opponent is, he must fall if he can be once robbed of his balance and prevented from recovering. From this basic statement of efficiency have evolved distinctive techniques of throwing and preparatory movements peculiar to judo.

Kano favoured a second maxim to express the value to society as a whole of judo practice: *jita kyoyei*. As with all maxims, detail is sacrificed for convenience and it suffers in translation. The conventional translation is 'mutual benefit', but Geoffrey Gleeson, for many years National Coach to the BJA, has pointed out that the literal meaning is 'self-profit, mutual benefit'. He argues that when Kano put the proposition in this way he was breaking new ground; in Japan the individual is only important as part of a group. As society is nothing more than the sum total of its individual members, Kano was plainly saying that it (and therefore everyone) benefited from individual advancement. Such personal advancement is a strong feature of Kodokan judo.

The philosophy pursued in judo practice is a matter for the individual. Ju-jutsu was a *samurai* art and entailed a devotion to practice consistent with the precepts of **bushido**. The *samurai* ethic has been heavily romanticized and it is even said that **bushido** is largely a distillation of *samurai* culture done with the benefit of hindsight; whatever the true position, there is no doubt that exceptional sincerity was required of a trainee, and Zen Buddhist philosophy, with its apparent contempt for things of this world, perfectly suited the **esprit de corps**. The *samurai* did not tread the path to *nirvana* (perfect understanding), he trod the path of **bushido** (perfect warriorhood). He was a knight, not a saint.

Zen has a subtle flavour; it cannot be tasted so long as the mind proceeds from assumption, prejudice and conceptual distinctions. Reality is the only fact; all else is assumption; act accordingly. The zen master and swordsman Odagiri Ichiun (*c* 1600) gave clear instructions:

When with a sword you confront the enemy, if the distance is too far, advance toward him and strike. When from the first the distance is just right, strike him from where you are. No thinking is needed.*

Attempts to rationalise a situation add a further dimension to it. Thus:

With most swordsmen, however, the case is different. As soon as they stand against the enemy, they fix their glance on him; survey the distance between them; take up the position which they think will be most advantageous; measure the length of the sword; reflect on what kind of technical trickeries they will use – 'giving', 'taking away' or 'slowing of motion' and so on. Their mind works in the busiest way possible on how best to make use of all the tactics they have learned. They have no idea whatever of Heavenly Reason and its functioning under varying conditions.

Reality is a shapeless unity; the mind which discriminates between aspects of it sees only disunity; remain unconcerned;

The great mistake in swordsmanship is to anticipate the outcome of the engagement; you ought not to be thinking of whether it ends in victory or in defeat. Just let the Nature take its course, and your sword will strike at the right moment.

The philosophy contained in these few paragraphs is all-embracing. Every moment of life, and not just the judo moments, can afford a glimpse of Ichiun's reality. It is a philosophy for the judo player who is philosophical in his everyday affairs also. A narrower view is adopted by the great majority of players; they regard practice as a process of evolution in which the body is

kept fit and the mind stimulated.

Randori (free practice) is not mere repetition. Judo movements can be combined in a limitless variety of ways and every two players carve out an original sequence between them whenever they meet. Apart from being good exercise, *randori* is never monotonous; its pace and intensity are worked out by the two players according to their age, sex, strength, size and ambitions. This means that there is always a level of judo appropriate to youth, womanhood, age, blindness, childhood or any other disposition with physical implications.

A player is both attacker and defender simultaneously in *randori.* On the one hand he must employ strategy, agility, strength and judgement; on the other he must be alert, quick-witted, self-disciplined and cautious. These factors are of immense value in any situation in which self-defence is used, and this is a common reason for beginning a study of judo. The truth is, however, that there are more effective methods of self-defence than judo, and although it has a contribution to make in that direction the real value of the sport lies in its ability to give personal satisfaction. The benefit of progress in judo is confidence, and the lesson it teaches is humility and respect. In the right proportions these qualities instil 'character' and as a competitive, safe sport, judo is a means of fulfilment for those who practice it.

CHAPTER 4.   THE DOJO, ETIQUETTE AND CONVENTIONS

The focal point of all judo activity is the *dojo* (training hall). It is here that players at every level of ability strive towards their personal objectives by practising and improving upon their hard-won skills. Judo training schools are no longer closed societies, but it is still true that the judo encountered in one *dojo* can vary considerably

from that encountered in another. Skill in judo is only acquired by practice and study, and in the right environment the standards that can be reached are limitless.

There is no stereotype of what a *dojo* should look like. Structurally, the ideal is a quiet, spacious hall equipped with a permanent mat area. There must

be no sharp protrusions close to the mat, the ceiling must be high enough (4m +) to allow full-blooded throwing, and a resilient floor beneath the mats is preferable to a solid concrete one. It is well worth travelling in order to train at a *dojo* which combines these amenities with good shower and changing facilities.

*(from **Zen and Japanese Culture**, D T Suzuki, Routledge & Kegan Paul and Princeton University Press)

THE DOJO, ETIQUETTE AND CONVENTIONS

The most important item of equipment in a *dojo* is the mat area. Japanese *tatami* (tightly woven straw mats about 2m x 1m x 6cm) are popular, having a vinyl top surface (usually green) and a non-slip underside. They are pushed together to provide a firm, fast and level mat area which is at the same time sufficiently yielding to prevent a *judoka* (judo player) from being hurt when thrown. Some mat areas in Japan are made up of five hundred or more of these *tatami*, but for basic requirements an area in excess of 10m square is adequate.

For many years Japanese *tatami* were thought to be the last word in judo mats. Latterly, however, modern materials have exposed the limitations of woven straw and have shown that traditional *tatami* are only suitable for a *dojo* with a sprung floor. These are universal in Japan where buildings are constructed with due regard for the risk of earth tremors. Experimentation with polymers and plastic foam has produced a universally acceptable mat; there is cogent evidence that its use has dramatically reduced the incidence of injury in

Randori at a modern European *dojo,* that of the London Judo Society.

competition, and the latest mats are so advanced that Japanese *tatami* have not been used in the last two Olympics or in the last five World Championships.

The principal stumbling block to widespread use of the best mats is cost; for economy many *dojo* use rubber or foam undermats kept in position by a wooden frame and covered by a tightly-stretched canvas sheet. This system is perfectly acceptable provided the canvas is kept taut and the under mats stay firm beneath the players' feet. *Judoka* who train on unduly soft mats risk injury to toes, ankles and knees; they will also perform slower judo than their counterparts who use a firm surface.

Nowadays a progressive *dojo* will contain a number of ancillary training aids in addition to a good mat area. A set of weights is a common sight, especially in a *dojo* whose members aspire to competition honours, and sometimes, for use at all levels, a large mirror is positioned to give coverage of the mat; by practising a movement in front of it a player can spot any glaring errors in his technique. Tyre inner tubes are also useful: when fastened to a wall or pillar at chest height they can be gripped as an opponent would be gripped for the purpose of practising the hand and foot positioning of a given throw. Increasingly popular is the gymnasium crash mat which enables a player to polish a clumsy throwing technique by repetition, allowing his opponent a soft landing every time. Visual aids such as cine projectors and video tape recorders are found to be very useful by the few clubs that can afford to hire them.

The personal equipment needed by a *judoka* consists of his *judogi* and a pair of *zori* (toe-grip straw sandals) for off-the-mat wear. A *judogi* consists of jacket, belt and trousers in heavy-duty cotton twill reinforced at the stress points.

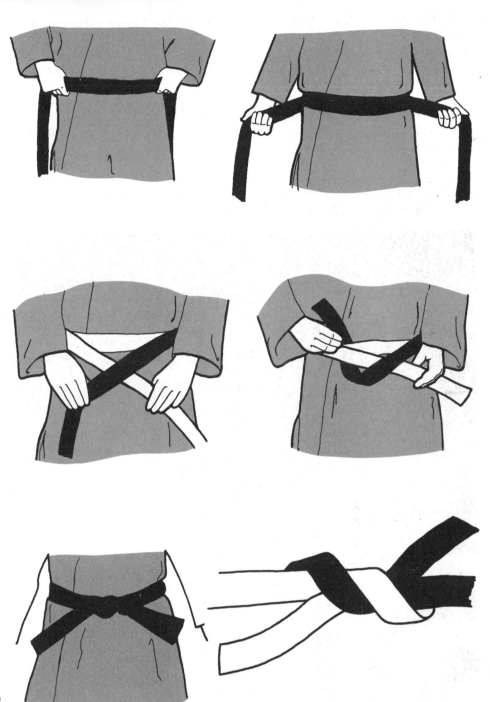

Belt Tying:
Take the belt in both hands and find its midsection.
Pass it once around the waist from the front as shown and bring the ends together again.

The knot is begun by feeding the outer belt end underneath all the wrapped around sections of belt. It is finished by tying the two free ends together in the first half of a reef knot. The belt should be tied reasonably tightly to prevent it coming undone.

The suit must be white or slightly off white in colour. For a proper fit the trousers must reach below the knees and the jacket below the elbows sufficiently far to keep them covered during practice. Women and girls are expected to wear a tee shirt (or leotard) beneath their jackets, but it is incorrect for men and boys to do so without a special reason. The traditional view is that nothing should be worn beneath the trousers although the almost universal practice now is to wear swimming trunks or an athletic support. Certainly no player of either sex should wear any form of personal jewellery on the mat, because to do so would be dangerous for other players.

It is unusual for a *dojo* to be furnished or decorated other than in a simple way which reflects its purpose as a place of study. There is usually a general noticeboard and in some *dojo* there is a board on which members' names are displayed against an indicator of their current grade. The principal feature of decoration symbolizes the aims and objectives of judo training. Commonly it takes the form of a picture of Kano or Koizumi; alternatively it might be a scroll or embroidery on which certain calligraphy, such as the characters meaning 'austere practice', appears.

Whatever form it takes, the part of the *dojo* in which it is situated is known as the *kamiza* (upper seat) and is regarded as the senior side of the hall. The side opposite is correspondingly called the *shimoza* (lower seat) and is usually the direction from which the mat must be approached. On entering or leaving the *dojo* the proper procedure is for every *judoka* to perform a standing bow *(ritsurei)* towards the *kamiza.*

Although a *dojo* is both a gymnasium and a club, it is primarily the place where a *judoka* trains to achieve certain objectives. Those objectives

vary according to individual ambitions, but in every case the progress actually made towards achieving them reflects the atmosphere that prevails. It is no coincidence that famous *dojo* have high standards.

The standard of conduct followed in modern clubs tends not to follow the traditional pattern of etiquette. Most experienced *judoka* are aware of the pattern but it is not adhered to consistently and some people regret this. In judo, etiquette is merely another word for courtesy. The courtesy required in judo takes the form of gestures of respect for other *judoka* and for the aims of judo training itself.

One example of this respect has already been given: bowing when entering and leaving the *dojo.* Once the principle behind the gesture is appreciated, the other aspects of etiquette can be readily understood. Thus, long toe or finger nails, a dirty suit, smoking in the *dojo* and sprawling about on the mat

when other *judoka* are training are out of order. Talking during practice must be avoided because it is distracting and because there is a risk of biting the tongue. The class ought to be opened and closed formally with the instructors lined up in order of seniority opposite the pupils similarly lined up, each side performing a kneeling bow *(zarei)* to the other when the command is given. It is wrong for trainees to disrupt a session by coming to the mat late or leaving early without first obtaining the permission of the instructor in charge, and it is proper to bow to any opponent, without exception, before and after any form of practice with him. If an opponent performs an outstanding *waza* (technique) in practice it is appropriate to show respect for his achievement by bowing. Skill in judo does not happen by accident; for that reason alone the pursuit of skill and its attainment deserve respect.

Zarei:

Kneeling bow. Adopt a kneeling position with hands flat on the thighs and body alert. The knees rest shoulder's width apart and the feet lie flat beneath the buttocks. Pause.

Place the hands flat on the mat with the fingers pointing inwards. Bow solemnly by lowering head and shoulders as one until the top of the forehead is towards the opponent. Pause. Rise up.

CHAPTER 5. THE GRADING SYSTEM

The belt system is a distinctive feature of judo. A player can test his ability by entering for examination within a system of grades, and by demonstrating superiority over a cross-section of players at the same level as himself he wins promotion to the next rank. In this way successive ranks become populated by increasingly skilful players until eventually all *judoka* who participate consistently are distributed throughout the hierarchy according to their proven ability.

The time-honoured distinction is between *kyu* (student) and *dan* (advanced) grades. Put simply, the distinction marks the point at which emphasis shifts away from the acquisition of technique on to its effective application. There are nine *kyu* grades in use and their designated colours are as follows:

9th *kyu*	yellow belt	*kukyu*
8th *kyu*	orange belt	*hakkyu*
7th *kyu*	orange belt	*shikkyu*
6th *kyu*	green belt	*rokkyu*
5th *kyu*	green belt	*gokyu*
4th *kyu*	blue belt	*yonkyu*
3rd *kyu*	blue belt	*sankyu*
2nd *kyu*	brown belt	*nikyu*
1st *kyu*	brown belt	*ikkyu*

A raw novice begins by wearing a plain white belt, but as soon as he has satisfactorily completed a course of elementary instruction at a recognized club, his instructor can, if registered, award him 9th *kyu* grade. Thereafter promotion up to 1st *kyu* must be earned by entering official promotion examinations: beyond 1st *kyu* promotion can be based in part on winning performances in certain other types of contest.

Promotion with the *dan* degree does not carry a change of designated colour until 6th *dan* is reached. Even then it is customary for the holder to continue wearing a black belt in everyday practice, reserving the official colour for ceremonial occasions. The *dan* grades are as follows:

1st *dan*	black	*shodan*
2nd *dan*	black	*nidan*
3rd *dan*	black	*sandan*
4th *dan*	black	*shidan* (yondan)
5th *dan*	black	*godan*
6th *dan*	alternating red and white blocks	*rokudan*
7th *dan*	alternating red and white blocks	*shichidan*
8th *dan*	alternating red and white blocks	*hachidan*
9th *dan*	red	*kudan*
10th *dan*	red	*judan*

Although examinations are held in the United Kingdom for promotion up to 5th *dan,* the *dan* grades beyond that are only awarded through the Executive Committee of the BJA.

In recent years the number of *dan* grades in regular practice has grown considerably, but even so the black belt remains a coveted symbol. It is the colour of the five fighting grades *par excellence* (1st *dan* through to 5th *dan*) and is awarded only to those who can demonstrate a high level of accomplishment in their judo. As a *judoka* closes the gap between 9th *kyu* and 1st *dan* he acquires technical proficiency, but that alone is not enough to put him in black. He must be able to defeat most competent *kyu* grades decisively in contest before he can cross the threshold from 1st *kyu* to 1st *dan.* An able beginner who trained with dedication under a good instructor might reach 1st *dan* in a little under two years. That would be exceptional; most people take considerably longer.

Contrary to popular belief, a *dan* grade does not automatically indicate teaching or coaching ability on the part of its possessor. It is true that a small number of *dan* degrees have been awarded for service to the sport (which can include teaching and coaching) but the great majority of grades up to 5th *dan* rest squarely on prowess in contest. The holder of a 5th *dan* is a player of extremely high calibre and he represents the pinnacle of competitive success. Higher *dan* grades are conferred on persons whose contribution and personal understanding outside the competitive sphere are exemplary. There have been seven 10th *dan* holders in the history of Kodokan judo (Kano never held a grade, there was no one to grade him), none of whom survive today. The status of the grade is near mythical and it represents a standard which is virtually unattainable.

Holders of 10th *dan* grade:

Hajime Isogai 1937*
Kaichiro Samura 1948
Hidekazu Nagaoka 1937*
Shotaro Tobata 1948
Kyuzo Mifune 1945
Yoshiaki Yamashita 1935*
Kunisaburo Iizuka 1946

*were awarded by Jigoro Kano.

Promotion by examination requires that a candidate should demonstrate practical ability and good theoretical knowledge. Practicability is tested by matching the examinee in contest with other examinees. Between 8th *kyu* and 1st *kyu* he must win at least one such contest in order to be eligible for promotion. At examinations for promotion to 1st *dan* and beyond a candidate is given two preliminary contests against his rivals. Should he win both, he is given a line-up of three opponents each of whom must be defeated in succession in order for him to qualify for the next grade.

For the theory part of the examination a knowledge of prescribed techniques and terminology is required. In a radical move the BJA recently abolished the theory requirement and allowed promotion entirely on contest ability. The result was that newcomers to the sport became increasingly ignorant of its finer points. In consequence a resolution for the reintroduction of a realistic theory element was approved by the BJA in 1977 and a syllabus has been drawn up accordingly.

Japanese terminology is an integral part of judo and an examiner expects the candidates to understand it fully. The language of judo is Japanese and *judoka* the world over are able to understand one another on the mat. Much of the terminology cannot be translated directly into sensible English and the beginner is best advised to build up a vocabulary in Japanese rather than risk the confusion of translation.

The techniques listed in the syllabus have been selected to provide a test of skill appropriate to the grade for which a candidate presents himself. The examiner must satisfy himself that the examinee can properly execute any of the movements listed at or below that grade. This he will do by requiring the demonstration of named holds or throws. The examinable techniques become increasingly sophisticated until by the time 1st *dan* is reached the syllabus

has covered every important move in the judo repertoire.

In order to derive maximum benefit from the grading structure as a yardstick of ability a trainee should draw certain conclusions from the way it operates. First, high-grade players exhibit the skills required to progress; they should never be avoided simply because they win easily; the bulk of free practice should be with them. Second, the system provides an objective assessment of competence; every promotion examination should be entered regardless of personal opinion about the outcome; failure to go up a grade means that a black belt will have been earned when received. Third, the right preparation for success in contest is the study and analysis of technique; winning merely follows on from that.

BELT RANKS

The belt grading system in the United States has retained the traditional six *kyu* grades before attainment of a black belt, instead of the ten *kyu* grades used for judo in the United Kingdom. Requirements for promotion in the United States are fulfilled by spending proper time in grade, by understanding Japanese

terminology and the history of judo, by having knowledge of contest rules, by demonstrating techniques and forms, and by accumulating promotion points. Understanding judo theory is not directly asked or required; however, demonstration of techniques includes combination and counter moves which illustrate judo theory.

Today in the United States, there are various paths to rank promotion. Promotion points are accumulated for both competition and service to judo. Service points are given for being an instructor, a clinic host, a tournament director, and other task oriented judo service.

Conflicting opinions currently exist concerning the time in grade required for competitors versus noncompetitors. There is also a debate concerning the number of promotion points which can be earned through competition versus those which can be earned through service. At present, the length of time in grade and the number of promotion points required are the same for both the competitor and the non-competitor. However, this is now being reviewed and may be changed to increase the requirement standards for the noncompetitive class.

CHAPTER 6.   BASIC SKILLS

Progress in judo rests on two related abilities. The first is the ability to acquire technical proficiency, the second to apply that proficiency as and when appropriate. The correct application of technique requires a variety of qualities best summarized as presence of mind. This is the ingredient which enables one player to beat an equally competent opponent; a *judoka* at 1st *kyu* level has the same building blocks at his disposal as a 5th *dan*, but he is unable to assemble them for use as readily when an opportunity presents itself. The solution here

is the long-term one of building up a large bank of experience.

Every course of instruction begins with breakfalls *(ukemi)*. The correct approach to throwing requires fluid movement and commitment, neither of which can be achieved by someone who is terrified of being thrown. By learning how to fall without discomfort, fear is eliminated and the beginner is introduced to the unfamiliar feeling of movement in an upside down position. Lest it be thought that breakfalls are strictly for beginners, it should also be pointed out that breakfall

practice is required of all grades during preliminary exercises at the top *dojos.*

According to Newton, to every action there is an equal and opposite reaction; when a body hits the ground, the ground seems to be hitting back proportionately. In the case of a rubber ball, the impact is rendered harmless by a bouncing response. An egg, on the other hand, is brittle and maximizes the harm of impact by smashing on contact. It is clear from these analogies that the aim in falling is to imitate rubber by keeping the body flexible and

Backwards Breakfall:

Sit relaxed with arms stretched forwards and palms turned down. Bend the knees slightly.

Tuck the chin in by looking at the belt so that the back becomes rounded. Raise both legs and roll backwards.

Just before the shoulder blades touch the mat, slap downwards with palms and forearms. Do not reach for the mat prematurely; do not let the head move from its tucked-in position.

Standing Backwards Breakfall:

As confidence increases the backwards breakfall can be done from a standing position.

Tuck the head in as before and round the shoulders by raising the arms at the front.

Drop the body by sitting down and rolling smoothly backwards just before the buttocks meet the mat.

Remember to raise the legs and keep the head up. Slap downwards, visualizing the arms as lengths of flexible hosepipe.

27

Forward Breakfall:

Begin in an upright kneeling position with the toes turned up. Raise the forearms with palms turned down.

Allow the body to fall forwards along its length.

Without reaching out for the ground, slap downwards with the palms and forearms just soon enough to avoid touching the mat with any other part of the upper body.

As confidence increases the exercise can be performed, through stages, from a fully-standing position.

relaxed. As a further refinement, the judo method of falling adopts the principle that the impact of landing need not be received by the whole body but can instead be accommodated by a more convenient part of it, namely the arm. The human body as a whole cannot bounce, but a rope-like arm can and does.

The shock of landing is dissipated in judo either by rolling out of a throw or by diverting it into a harmless response. A roll is possible when the hand or upper arm can be placed to the ground first, as shown; this commonly occurs in throws such as *tomoenage.* In every other situation, the breakfall is performed by

slapping the *tatami* with the whole arm, palm of the hand downwards, momentarily before the body weight lands. This means that the arm concerned is accelerated to overtake the trunk at the last moment of the fall. Once efficiency is achieved, progressively complex falling exercises can be used to build confidence.

Side Breakfall:

Squat in an upright position with one leg stretched comfortably out in front. Raise the arm on the same side to shoulder height and hold it half across the chest. The other hand holds the belt.

Allow the body to fall gently backwards. Push down a little with the support foot so that the body rolls onto the opposite side of the back. Breakfall with the free arm.

Repeat the exercise on both sides. Keep the head up by looking at the belt.

Standing Side Breakfall:

Prepare the upper body as before. Step diagonally across the body with one leg. Do not replace the foot on the ground; simply continue to stretch it out forwards and go down on the support leg, as shown. Roll backwards before the buttocks touch the mat.

Again, by pressing down slightly with the support leg the back will be turned down onto the opposite side. Slap downwards decisively; keep the head up.

It often happens that in a perfectly executed throw the loser lands flat on his back at some speed. Although this will seem to be a heavy fall, it is completely painless. In fact seasoned players do not even bother to breakfall as such when this happens. They simply gather themselves up by holding their bodies firm (*not* bracing them) in order to prevent a sprawling landing with the legs and head. The head is incapable of rebounding like an arm and must always be kept clear of the mat. This must be achieved by practising breakfalls with the eyes fixed firmly on the knot at the front of the belt until the position becomes a reflex. Although the legs are not such good shock absorbers as the arms, they have a role to play in co-ordinating a fall; rather than cause confusion by teaching leg-involvement at the outset, the student is left to develop the knack of his own accord.

Having spent a short time on breakfalls, the novice is then given instruction in *nagewaza* (throwing techniques) and *katamewaza* (groundwork techniques). There are no secrets involved; the movements are mechanical and can be learned by anyone. *Nagewaza*

are sub-divided into five categories in which throws are grouped according to their dominant feature:

(1) *Tewaza* (hand and arm techniques)
(2) *Koshiwaza* (hip and trunk techniques)
(3) *Ashiwaza* (foot and leg techniques)
(4) *Masutemiwaza* (backwards falling throws)
(5) *Yokosutemiwaza* (sideways falling throws)

Katamewaza are sub-divided into three categories:

(1) *Osaekomiwaza* (hold downs)
(2) *Kansetsuwaza* (arm locking techniques)
(3) *Shimewaza* (strangulation techniques)

Detailed instructions for performing a wide range of judo techniques are given in Parts 3 and 4. The classic analysis applicable to all throws is that they are continuous movements comprising three key elements. Unless all are present a throw will fail. *Kuzushi* is the element of imbalance. Whenever the

body weight ceases to fall squarely on both feet a state of relative imbalance exists. Ultimate imbalance occurs when an opponent's weight is on neither foot, i.e. he is being thrown. *Tsukuri* describes the process of adopting the correct posture for a given throw; it covers the mechanical aspects of a technique. This process may of itself create imbalance in an opponent, e.g. *seoinage,* or it may take advantage of his partial imbalance by preventing a recovery, e.g. *deashiharai. Kake* is the stage when a throw goes beyond the point of no return. It consists in applying technique so as to put an opponent to the mat with impetus but under control.

In order to practice judo in *randori* or contest a beginner needs to appreciate that his opponent's movements dictate the course of events just as much as his own do. The *status quo* is mutual balance. Before taking hold, each stands in a

29

Rolling Breakfall:

Stand with the feet comfortably apart.

Bend down and place one hand palm down on the mat with the fingers pointing forwards. Tuck the head in by looking at the belt.

Turn the other arm inwards and place the hand palm down on the mat between the feet with the

perfectly balanced posture. This is either *shizenhontai* (natural posture), in which the arms rest easily at the side of the body and the feet stand shoulders' width apart; or *migishizentai* (right natural posture), in which the right foot is slightly advanced; or

hidarishizentai (left natural posture), in which the left foot is slightly advanced. Upon taking hold, individual balance becomes in varying degrees dependent on the actions of the opponent so long as a handhold is maintained.

The purpose in taking hold

(kumikata) is to generate movement and to gain control of a partner's impetus. The conventional grip is with the right hand at his left lapel and the left hand at the elbow of his right sleeve. A good habit to get into is that of closing the grip with the second, third and fourth

Kumikata: Methods of gripping:

The conventional hold; one hand on the lapel at chest height, the other controlling the opponent's other side with a grip at the sleeve behind and just above the elbow.

A double lapel grip: gives incomplete control but facilitates a rapid switch from an attack on one side to an attack on the other. Made more effec- tive by plucking at the opponent's jacket until a 'flap' appears in it below his collar bone and then holding the flap so produced. One hand high on the collar with the other holding the opposite sleeve low down the forearm: this grip is much favoured by *uchimata* special- ists because it can be used to induce a forward-leaning stoop in the opponent's posture.

Double sleeve grip: though not seen very often nowa- days, it has its uses in, for example, *tsurikomigoshi* on either side and the long-distance style *okuriashiharai*.

Confuses grizzly- bear opponents who want close combat and can unsettle them into error. Valuable as a source of irritation for the opponent.

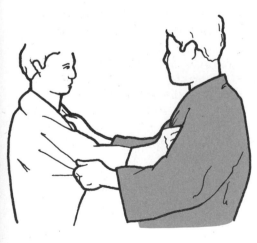

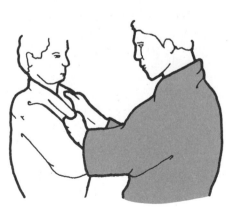

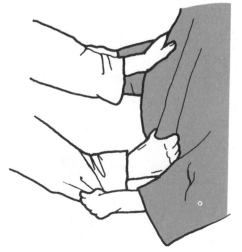

fingers pointing backwards. Slide this latter hand backwards along the mat a little until the body feels as though it wants to move forwards over it.

Roll easily over the curve created by the stretched arm and shoulders. Keep the head tucked in. The breakfall ends by slapping the mat with the free arm. Practice the fall on both sides.

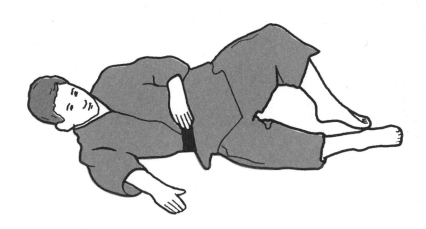

fingers before curling the first finger; this is stronger than relying on a predominantly first-finger-and-thumb grip. Although the conventional hold gives good control it is by no means obligatory. It is in fact a great weakness that in competition many players take a conventional hold without thinking about it and then lapse into routine moves that they habitually perform from such a position. Holding both sleeves or both lapels is acceptable and the right (or left) hand can, if preferred, grip the partner's collar at the nape of the neck or hold his jacket at the back by passing over or under his left (or right) arm. Experimentation with different holds is useful, especially for gaining experience of right-handed and left-handed throwing. The only prohibitions are that a player may not move about the mat with his hands both holding the same side of his partner's jacket and that he may not hold the jacket below the top of the side vent. For the express purpose of attempting a throw the belt may be gripped, the jacket may be held on the same side with two hands, and the trouser leg may be grasped for the duration of a single pace. At no time in

standing judo is a player permitted to hold with his fingers inside his opponent's *judogi.*

When grasped the opponent will react in one of several ways. He may crouch down in a strong defensive posture *(jigotai)*; he may try to break the grip and secure his own preferred hold; he may move about with stiff straight arms to hold off attacks or he may move freely into attacking sequences of his own. The general proposition is that his reaction must be used to produce an over reaction and should not be accepted at face value. Movement must be pressed on him until he cannot cope.

Care must be taken not to move haphazardly during free

practice. Walking is a momentary loss of balance followed by a rapid recovery and so far as possible it is desirable to keep the body weight spread evenly between both feet. This gives rise to a form of judo shuffle in which short steps are taken, avoiding up and down movement by walking from the hip, with the soles of the feet barely clearing the mat. When a full pace is taken with each foot successively the progression is called *ayumi ashi* (normal walking); when one foot leads at every pace and the trailing foot follows without passing, the progression is called *tsugi ashi* (following foot walking). It is unwise to take big sweeping steps in judo or to move in predictable sequences.

Sooner or later every *judoka* is obliged to consider the role of strength in judo. Strength divorced from skill is a corruption of judo, but there is a body of opinion which holds that 'pure judo' involves skill divorced from strength. Not everyone agrees. The resulting controversy is important because it affects the individual's attitude to training in matters such as weight training and exposure to contest.

The 'pure judo' proposition harks back to first principles. *Ju* is not an easy principle to translate into English, and various translations such as 'sleight of body', 'pliability' and 'non-resistance' have been used to convey the meaning. Kano himself regularly used the phrase 'non-resistance'; moreover he illustrated the concept by examples which have been relied on by theorists for the assertion that strength is surplus to skill. Thus: if X, who possesses 10 units of strength, pushes against Y, who possesses only 7 units, and Y tries to stand his ground, X will succeed in driving him backwards. Should Y suddenly reverse the direction of his effort, however, there will be anything up to 17 units carrying X towards him. X's impetus turns into momentum and Y can throw him effortlessly as he crashes past.

In the example given the amount of strength employed need not be very great in order to throw the attacker convincingly. It is most important to realise, though, that X has conceded all the impetus necessary for such an outcome. Experienced judo players do not make any concessions in contest, nor should they if it is to be a test of ability. This gives rise to a fundamental distinction between *randori* and contest. In *randori*, the players are willing to move freely so that emphasis can be placed on the development of skill; in contest there has to be an additional input of effort to smother an opponent's obstructiveness. That explains why weight categories are now in general use and why there never has been a small All-Japan Champion in the history of judo. Contest judo is not inferior judo. It is an elaboration on the 'purer' judo expressed in *randori*, but the skill remains the same.

Uchikomi (winding-in) practice is designed to give trainees mastery of the body movements used in different throws. The *tsukuri* of a given throw is practiced without *kake*. With the help of a partner, or by using rubber tubes, a *judoka* repeatedly swings in for a throw and brings it to the point of execution before easing off and withdrawing to his starting position. The aim is to produce a fluent reflex by repetition. The first stage establishes a coherent sequence, the second brings speed into play and at the third stage the partner increases his resistance in order to test the efficiency of the movement. When the pre-arranged number of repetitions has been performed (100 per throw, four or five throws, is not excessive at serious levels), one full throw is executed to finish off.

Randori introduces movement into the study of technique. At one extreme it is *uchikomi* on the move as when both throw and thrower are predetermined; at the other it is free sparring not far short of contest. If the full value of *randori* is to be realized it must be practised without violence. As clubs become increasingly 'contest conscious', there is a temptation for the players to put something at stake in *randori* and turn it into an off-the-cuff contest. This should be avoided so that for training purposes an atmosphere in which people can throw and be thrown without loss of face is created. That way players can learn to recognize opportunities as they occur while continuing to enjoy their judo. As a matter of courtesy, strong vigorous male players should moderate their practice when paired with adolescents, women and older men, all of whom have a right not to be caught up in a preparation for the next Olympics!

Just as contest adds noncooperation to *randori,* so *kata* (formal demonstration) adds full co-operation.

There are ten *kata* presently in widespread use in various Western countries, although they have become a neglected aspect of judo training. The ten are:

(1) *Nagenokata* (forms of throwing)
This is a tableau of fifteen throws demonstrated to the left and right hand sides. Five groups of three throws illustrate different aspects of *nagewaza*.

(2) *Katamenokata* (forms of groundwork)
A tableau of groundwork techniques. Fifteen techniques are shown, five from each of the three sub-divisions of *katamewaza*.

(3) *Junokata* (forms of *Ju*)
A sequence of fifteen reactions to attack arranged in three sets to illustrate the principle of *Ju*.

(4) *Gonosennokata* (forms of counterthrowing)
A dynamic sequence of twelve attacks in which *tori* (the demonstrator) snatches the initiative from an attacker and throws him decisively.

(5) *Kimenokata* (forms of decision)
Twenty disabling moves arranged in two sets (eight and twelve respectively) variously directed against an assassin armed with a knife, sword or unarmed.

(6) *Koshikinokata* (ancient forms of throwing)
Highly stylized demonstration of twenty-one responses to attack derived from *ju-jutsu* methods which preceded judo.

(7) *Itsutsunokata* (form of five concepts)
An unfinished *kata* which attempts to capture and portray the precise moment at which presence of mind causes the

downfall of an opponent. More subtle than *junokata* and esoteric in flavour.

(8) *Sciryokuzenyo Kokumintaiiku* (national physical exercise based on the principle of maximum efficiency)
The complete repertoire involves 36 set pieces in three groups: 16 striking and kicking actions; 10 attacks; 10 pliable responses.

(9) *Goshinjutsunokata* (self-defence *kata* for men)
Not used in the UK, but one of the official Kodokan *kata*.

(10) *Joshigoshinho* (self-defence *kata* for women)
Dating from *c.* 1940 and formulated at the suggestion of Kano's nephew, this is a *kata* of 18 movements in three parts: 8 basic patterns; 5 methods of escape; 5 methods of retaliation.

Items 8, 9 and 10 are not used in the UK; item 4 is not used in the USA, though widely used in Europe, and is not an official Kodokan *kata*.

These *kata* are a judo catechism; they are stylized presentations in which correctness of the chosen form is paramount. There is little room for improvization and the format is ritualized to direct attention to the subtleties of posture, distance, co-ordination and presence of mind. Both *tori* and *uke* (the person thrown) act in unison. Together they make a concerted effort to stage an interpretation of principle. Properly performed, *kata* can give a feel for the deeper side of judo and they are a valuable exercise for older players because of the restraint they embody. Improperly performed, they are a jumble of technique and ritual.

The methods of practice outlined above are used to develop skill in *judoka* who have a basic knowledge of the building blocks involved. A good basic knowledge is readily obtained, but in order to avoid wasting effort an advanced player needs proper guidance

just as much as a beginner. Players used to make their own way beyond 1st *kyu*, each crop of students managing to raise the overall standard a little higher than the last. With the advent of Olympic competition it became apparent that high-level coaching would have to be made available if talent was not to go to waste. To that end the BJA appointed a full-time national coach in 1960 and took action to build up a corps of coaches at club and area levels able to communicate knowledge and manage training sessions effectively. The advanced player now has access to all the guidance he needs to improve still further. All that is required of him is that he keep an open mind, listen to experienced coaches and retain some humility.

Kata in the United States is generally not emphasized as a part of judo training. Most judoka tend to only study or perform *kata* prior to a belt examination. *Kata* in other martial arts is heavily utilized for training by both *kyu* and *dan* grades. In judo, the late entry into study of *kata*, usually at the brown belt level, is probably one reason for low judoka interest. *Kata* training after a few years of *randori* practice seems dull, uninteresting, and irrelevant to competitive judo training.

Another reason for low jukoka interest in *kata* is that *kata* has not evolved with time to meet the current needs of modern judo. The original purpose of *kata* was to give a prearranged sequence of events in which optimum execution of techniques can be used and studied. *Kata* related to an ideal situation and taken out of a hypothetical contest or self defense situation, is used to illustrate better timing, tempo, off balance, etcetera. As time has passed in the development of judo, old *kata* has many times remained as a highly stylized representation of

what judo was during the latter half of the nineteenth century. The inability of judo leaders to update *kata* training and give relevance to its purpose has left it as a minor aspect of judo in the United States.

Mini-kata or *uchikomi* has generally taken the place of formal *kata* training in judo instruction. The main problem with the utilization of *uchikomi* at the exclusion of *kata* is that it isolates a portion of the ideal structure from the sequence of events that *kata* training offers. This inadequacy of traditional *uchikomi* has given rise to drill training or moving *uchikomi*. Drill training tends to be the halfway point between traditional *kata* and *randori* training.

Drill training emphasizes dynamic movement rather than static training like traditional *uchikomi*; in this respect, it represents the original function of *kata*. On the other hand, drill training or moving *uchikomi* offers a variable degree of the non-predictability of *randori* or *shiai*. The mixing of the traditional training areas of *kata* and *randori* has further developed other marginally different training methods.

Another variation is the performance of traditional *kata* under *randori* conditions. This modification creates a new method of bridging the gaps which exist between learning a technique and being able to apply the technique in a competitive or self defense situation. *Randori-styled kata* is traditional *kata* which has not been ritualized to the point of exact precise movements. Instead, the movements which lead up to execution resemble two judoka who are engaged in *randori* or *shiai*.

If *kata* in judo is to be useful and to become a widely utilized method of training, it must be dynamic, and possess a potential for interchangable variables. There must be new kata developed to fit current competitive needs. The Gonosennokata is an example of a non-traditional kata utilizing countering techniques. This kata is virtually unknown in the United States.

CHAPTER 8. MENTAL DEVELOPMENT

Kano was an educationalist and his statement of judo objectives reflected this. In these, judo is a sophisticated physical art which can stimulate and satisfy an enquiring mind. There is scope for an athletic player to train towards prowess in contest and equally there is scope for a philosophical player to glimpse through judo the reality which is eluding him. Judo will not turn an athlete into a philosopher against his will, but to the extent that an individual has the capacity for insight there is depth enough to satisfy him.

Insight is an emotive term. The oriental view is that progress in any martial art concerns mind and body. Simply because the body is tangible is no reason to neglect the intangible benefits claimed for mental development. When contest days are over there would be nothing left if winning in competition were the sole purpose of judo training.

Breath control is not taught in judo dojo. Many Japanese dojo make it a habit to sit quietly in zazen (sitting meditation) for several minutes at the beginning and end of a session, but the practice is not widespread in Europe. The teaching that breath control is an avenue towards mental awareness is based on observation. Man can survive without food for many days, without water for less and without air for a mere four minutes. Anger is attended by inflamed breathing, serenity by tranquil breathing. The premise is that a controlled breathing pattern will subdue passion and give access to thought processes.

Contemplation is not a static exercise in the context of judo. Ever-changing patterns of movement insist that if reality is to be grasped it will be intuitively, not logically. The equivalent of Ichiun's swordsmanship in judo is the throw which occurs without any decision having been taken to attempt it. Every judoka has this experience from time to time. An opportunity presents itself; the thrower intuitively realizes and strikes without the hindrance of calculated effort. The timing is right of its own accord.

A stranger to a judo dojo soon notices that at moments of psychological tension some players yell out loud as they wring the last drop of energy from their bodies. The cry is spontaneous and is called a kiai. It shatters an opponent's presence of mind and physically tightens the muscles of the lower trunk, making extra strength available. The sound is unmistakable as an expression of commitment torn from the heart, guts and mind by the pressure of the moment.

In classical terms the vitality (ki) received from inspired air abides in the saikatanden, an area of the lower abdomen. It is psychic energy likened to volume upon volume of massed water. The mind has the power to release its potential and lead the flow through the limbs of the body so long as they remain pliable and receptive. A kiai is part of the escape of energy expressed as sound. Awareness of ki is experienced by breathing in fully and allowing the abdomen to expand roundly outwards. As the attention of the mind settles on the abdomen beneath the navel, a tingling sensation is felt; there is a little surge of warmth and a feeling of being uplifted briefly. On breathing out, a wave of vitality ebbs through the muscles.

Modern judo is not a martial art in the samurai sense. Nevertheless its rules do provide for a symbolic death in the form of an outright win by ippon (full point). No injury is caused, but in terms of contest such a defeat is absolute and crushing. Likewise in spirited practice a volley of attack and counterattack can climax in the style of mortal combat. There is correspondingly a level of mental awareness appropriate to the situation. Ichiun used the phrase aiuchi (mutual striking down) to describe it. It means:

Paying no attention whatever to the outcome of the contest, being not at all concerned with the question of coming out of it safely or not. When a man faces a deadly situation in this frame of mind, he is the most resolute, the most desperate, the most daring person, before whom no enemy can stand unless he himself has come to the same resolution.*

*(from Zen and Japanese Culture, D T Suzuki, Routledge & Kegan Paul and Princeton University Press)

The Gokyo

This list comprises the Gokyo plus the extra throws included in this book, and the groundwork techniques, titled in Japanese and English

The recognized and authoritative codification of throwing techniques in judo is known as the Gokyo; it stems from the original syllabus of Kodokan Judo. The Gokyo now consists of five sets or courses of throws, with eight techniques in each set. The sequence and grouping of these sets are arbitrary and can thus be confusing to the Westerner. In an attempt to assist an understanding of the inter-related throws we have modified the Gokyo in this book; related throws have been grouped together, starting with the simpler techniques and progressing to the more complex.

Judo enthusiasts, particularly beginners, should not study or practice more than one throw from each group at a time; to do otherwise will only result in confusion. The ideal is to work on the first throw of each group over months of practice, and only move on to the second in each group when the first have really been grasped. Try to study more than one throw of any group at a time and their particular essence will be lost.

All the techniques discussed here are depicted in a way that suits someone who favours the distinct right-hand stance, known as **migishizentai.** Most people are right-handed and so develop what is generally termed a 'right-handed technique'. Left-handed players who adopt the left stance should re-interpret the illustrations and commentary. Incidentally, being left-handed should not be considered a disadvantage: in fact a competitor with a distinct left-hand grip and stance and good throws on the left can be quite a force; his unusual inclination may make him more effective against right-handed opponents.

The player carrying out the technique and executing the throw is traditionally known as **tori**, the player being thrown as **uke**, (pronounced oo-key). These terms are used throughout this book.

At any time, some throws are more popular than others, whether at club, national or international level. This is quite natural: an instructor or champion may favour one particular technique and find that players copy him. Bear in mind, however, that a throw may not suit your temperament, build or general technique and use this book to widen your repertoire. Once you have mastered a basic throw, practice it with as many different people as possible. Build up a large range of throws. The competitor with just one powerful throw is eventually bound to meet an opponent with an even more powerful defence or, worse, a very fine counter technique **(kaeshiwaza).**

It is often said of judo that the more you learn the more fascinating it becomes. Repetition has not dulled the truth of this remark, as the rich variety of techniques in the following pages demonstrates.

Taiotoshi *(body drop)*

Of all the hand throws *taiotoshi* is probably the best for a beginner to start on. As is the case with most throws, there are a number of variations, but in all of them the basic action is the same. Competitors should be prepared to 'follow through' with their effort, for just as the golfer's swing does not stop when his club has struck the ball, so the good *judoka* should follow his action through to its conclusion.

The power of this action coupled with the footwork and body positioning should drive *uke* forward and over on to his right leg. There should be no hip or body contact. With feet well astride and balancing on both feet, *tori* should wheel his opponent around his own body and drop *uke* to the front.

Taiotoshi

As with most throws, good balance should be maintained in the early stages of *taiotoshi* to avoid being easily countered. *Tori* places his right foot between and just in front of *uke's* feet. Placing all his weight on that foot, he then spins his left foot back in a half circle with his heel leading and just brushing the mat with his toes, placing it just to the outside and slightly in front of *uke's* left foot. *Tori* should pull *uke's* right arm up and forward to *uke's* right-front corner and with his right arm well bent drive up and across under *uke's* chin, still maintaining his grip on *uke's* left lapel.

Tori must maintain his left-hand pull out and forward to prevent *uke* fending off *tori's* waist or hip with his hand. *Tori* should not pull down with his left hand into his own body for this throw. The whole action is completed as *tori* drives his own head and shoulders down and around to the left, looking right back behind him.

Neil Adams 3rd Dan

Junior European Champion, British Open Champion, West German Open Champion, Dutch Open Champion, All-England Champion.

Taiotoshi

Of this technique Neil says: 'It is my *tokuiwaza*, my favourite technique. I suppose I am very lucky in a way, *taiotoshi* being a throw that I both like and can do. I favour a particular style where I can get very low underneath the opponent — just as, I suppose, a *seoinage* specialist can get underneath his opponents. I especially like the whiplash effect that the finish of *taiotoshi* can provide and I have tried to perfect this.'

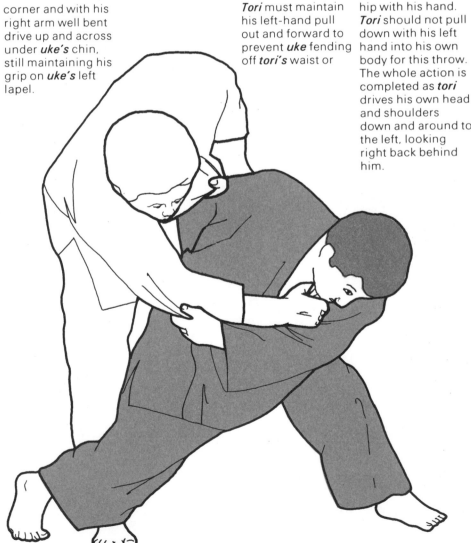

Seoinage *(shoulder throw)*

There are two distinct types of shoulder throw in use, *morote seoinage* (shoulder throw using both hands grip) and *ippon seoninage* (shoulder throw using a one hand grip). The latter is not listed in the Gokyo but is very popular at all levels of modern judo.

Seoinage is an arm throw, not a hip throw. A powerful impetus stems from the hands; *tori's* hips, although turned in deep, do not necessarily touch his opponent. It is a very difficult throw for *uke* to avoid or twist out of, and a clean throw ensures a score of *ippon.* Children love these throws, and the supple, turning, lifting action seems to suit most of them.

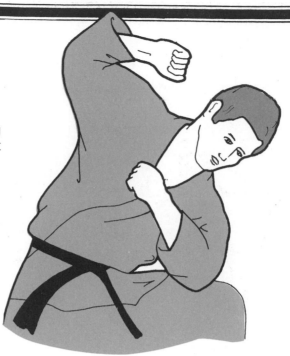

Morote seoinage

Using the normal right posture grips, *tori* makes his entry by jumping in and around, turning completely to land on both feet facing the same direction as *uke.* Co-ordination of hands and feet is essential with this throw. As *tori* jumps round to land with knees well bent, he must rock *uke's* upper weight forward on to the throw, tucking his right elbow through and between *uke's* left arm and trunk and driving his wrist high under *uke's* right armpit.

Tori should not strain his back by attempting to lift *uke* straight up but should rather bend forwards at his waist, straightening his legs.

Tori then throws *uke* across his upper back by tucking his head down and turning it to the left so that he is looking back behind *uke.* The tight arm lock ensures that *uke* cannot turn out of the throw. As he completes the throw, *tori's* own weight should lean into the direction of the throw and he should be well forward on his toes. If he were to rock back on his heels during the crucial moment of the throw, his opponent could 'block' the action and might follow through with a counter-technique.

40

Raymond Neenan, 3rd Dan
Twice British Open Champion, European Team Championships silver medallist.

Ippon Seoinage
'My particular style of *ippon seoinage* is the dropping style. Though I'm a lightweight, I am very tall and as generally other lightweights are shorter than me, they assume that I cannot get in low enough and usually bend forward at my initial attack. I find that by dropping to my knees they are caught in the trap. This is the style that brings me my success.'

Ippon seoinage

This throw is best done when *tori* is gripping *uke's* right sleeve just behind the elbow with his left hand, with knees well bent. *Tori* jumps in with a complete turn landing on both feet to face the same direction as *uke*.

Tori's right arm should lock high under *uke's* right armpit. His left foot must be tucked deep between *uke's* feet so that his right hip and buttock can turn across *uke's* right thigh.

To lift *uke* over the top, *tori* should bend forwards at his waist, jacking *uke* up with his hips. He should continue to tuck his head and right shoulder down to the mat, throwing his own head around to the left. He should

continue the follow-through action even when *uke* has gone over the top, since a clever opponent can easily twist out of the throw if there is not enough drive. *Tori* should throw his head round and look at the spot on which *uke* was originally standing.

Note that *tori's* right bicep should take the lift and that he should not turn in too deep with his shoulders. If *tori* tries to take the lift with his right shoulder it could be painful and would allow *uke* to counter the move with a standing strangle technique.

As he throws, *tori* should be rocking forward on his toes, not back on his heels.

Kataguruma

Tori must drop into a crouch position side on and at right angles to *uke*. He should drive his right arm between *uke's* legs and grip or lock on round and behind *uke's* right thigh. At the same time he should place his right foot between *uke's* feet, and with his left hand wrap *uke's* right arm across his shoulders and pull *uke* down to the mat.

As *uke's* feet lose contact with the mat, *tori* should slip *uke* over his head by dipping his head down sharply to the mat and at the same time straightening his legs from the crouch position.

Kataguruma *(shoulder wheel)*

The modern *kataguruma* is executed very quickly and with very little lift, quite unlike the original style. Though used infrequently, it produces dramatic results. *Tori* must exert a powerful left hand action to pull *uke* down and across his shoulders and wrap *uke's* right arm down, towards the mat.

A variation of this throw is also shown. *Tori* drops on to one knee and wheels his opponent over his shoulders rather than attempting a powerful lift.

Richard Barraclough, 4th Dan
Honorary National Coach, British and Universities international many times, holder of British titles in all styles of wrestling.

Kataguruma

'The technique I particularly like is *kataguruma,* the reason being that whenever we choose a favourite technique our build or body-type has something to do with it. This technique has particularly suited my body-type — I'm short but fairly heavy. The other thing I like about it really is that it is unorthodox, so it surprises people when you attack with it, which anyway gives you an initial advantage.'

Ukiotoshi *(floating drop)*

This throw is a good example of how an opponent's weight and broken balance can be used to best advantage. It is usually attempted when *uke* is pressing home an attack of his own and is already momentarily off balance to his right-front corner possibly after a flurry of action. Pure timing is essential in catching him at the right moment.

Driving powerfully his right hand through *uke's* upper chest and head and strongly twisting his upper body so that his right chest almost touches *uke's* left chest, *tori* also pulls down sharply with his left hand.

Ukiotoshi

As *uke* advances with his right foot, *tori* must step back widely on his left, at the same time pulling *uke's* right arm up and out in order to bring his opponent off-balance to his right-front corner. The co-ordinated pull-push of *tori's* hands is vital for the technique to succeed.

Uke is then wheeled over off his feet, *tori* thrusting strongly through *uke's* chest with his right arm.

Sumiotoshi *(corner drop)*

This throw is very similar to *ukiotoshi*, but this time *uke's* balance is broken towards his right-rear corner. Timing is again the essential ingredient. *Sumiotoshi* is the most difficult of the hand throws and as a result is rarely seen in competition; none the less it is as well to practice it regularly.

Many a contest against a difficult opponent has been won with a surprise technique such as this.

Both *ukiotoshi* and *sumiotoshi* have re-emerged in top-class international judo, in a much more dynamic and powerfully-executed style than when they were originally seen at such

levels. As top-class fighters become ever stronger and fitter throws are becoming more powerful and dynamic. Russian competitors in particular are quite adept at taking advantage of an opponent's weak balance and pull off these throws with devastating effect at the crucial moment.

Sumiotoshi

For this throw *tori* must catch *uke* off balance when both contestants are moving sideways and to *tori's* left. Bending at the knees (NOT at the waist), *tori* should advance his left foot well forward and to

the outside of *uke's* right foot, at the same time pulling *uke's* right elbow out to his right-rear corner and sharply down towards the mat.

While maintaining its grip on *uke's* left lapel, *tori's* right hand should drive through *uke's* chest and towards his right-rear corner. *Tori* does not turn in this throw, and drive into *uke's* right-rear corner should be maintained throughout.

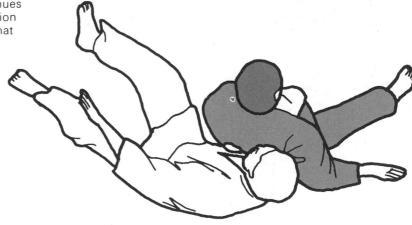

Sotomakikomi

Tori steps across *uke's* front with his right foot, landing just outside *uke's* right foot close to his little toe.

He then spins his left foot back between *uke's* feet, making a complete turn. As *tori* makes the turn he swings his right arm over the front of *uke's* forehead and locks tightly with his right elbow, tucking in and gripping *uke's* right arm.

Continuing the turn and going down to the mat if necessary, *tori* wheels his opponent over his back and continues the winding action down into the mat to finish with a perfect hold.

Sotomakikomi *(outer winding)*

Makikomi (winding) can be applied to a number of throws and, although looked upon with apprehension by some, is perfectly safe when applied correctly. *Uke* falls heavily from such a throw, and must breakfall not only for his own bodyweight but also for that of *tori. Makikomi* should not therefore be practised on or attempted with the inexperienced.

The footwork and turn-in for this throw is similar to that of *taiotoshi.* But in releasing his right-hand grip on *uke's* left lapel, *tori* wraps *uke* around himself and, with *uke* locked across his back, winds and twists forward and down into the mat. Being on the outside of *tori's* tight winding pivot, *uke* falls heavily and first to the mat. *Tori* must use space to launch

out into the roll or winding action down into the mat and must turn his head constantly to the left throughout the action. He should not fall to the mat like a log but rather wind himself right round so that finally he is looking at the spot where *uke* was originally standing.

45

Ogoshi *(major hip)*

This technique is very useful for beginners and enables them to learn how to get the full hip action for throws in the *koshi* family. Like the majority of throws in Chapter 10, these throws are also to *uke's* front, *tori* turning to face the same direction as *uke.* They also

involve *tori* throwing off both feet. The basic difference between this group of throws and others is that here *tori* uses his hip to lift or pick up *uke* and wheel him over.

In taking his right hip far across in front of *uke's* right thigh, it is essential for *tori* to get his opponent locked on to him for the throw by sliding his right arm around *uke's* back and pulling him on to him.

Ogoshi is not always practical for use against an experienced adversary, who will simply not allow the right arm to slip around his back; if he does so it will only be in order to effect an armlock. Nevertheless, this is a good 'opportunity throw' to be used when circumstances are right and should never be forgotten or discarded.

Ogoshi

Tori keeps his right arm free and grips with his left, at *uke's* right sleeve.

Tori then jumps round, both feet landing close together in between *uke's* feet. At the same time he must drive his right arm between *uke's* left arm and waist and seize *uke* around the middle, locking *uke's* body tightly to him.

Thrusting his hips past *uke's* right thigh and thus making a complete turn, *tori* should lift *uke* over his back by tucking his head and shoulders forward and down towards the mat and straightening his legs.

As soon as *tori* has successfully lifted *uke* across his back he should let his right arm go so that *uke* can be turned fully on to his back to avoid *uke's* weight bringing *tori* down as well.

Tsurigoshi *(lifting hip)*

Tori does not have to turn in so deep for this throw as for *ogoshi*, nor must he bend his knees so much. As for *ogoshi*, his right hand slips around the back but grips the belt, so as to get a powerful lift. **Tori** lifts his opponent up on to his hip rather than just locking his opponent to him. **Tori's** hips twist rather more on completion of the throw. Do not hold the belt too long before throwing, as this could result in a penalty.

Tsurigoshi

Virtually as in *ogoshi*, *tori* drives his right arm under *uke's* left arm and grips *uke's* belt at the back. Turning in at the same time to place his hips across *uke's* front, *tori* lifts *uke* on to his hip with a strong pull with the right arm. He completes the throw by wheeling *uke* over his lower back.

Koshiguruma

This throw looks very much the same as *ogoshi*. In both cases the hip of the thrower must go across the front of *uke's* hips and protrude well past. Instead of taking his right arm round *uke's* waist, however, as in *ogoshi, tori* should drive his right arm up and around *uke's* neck. Clamping it round *uke's* neck, *tori* should pull *uke* down across his hips and thus wheel *uke* over his lower back.

Koshiguruma *(hip wheel)*

The feet, leg and hip action of *koshiguruma* are much the same as for *ogoshi* and *tsurigoshi*. This throw depends however, on the right arm going up and around the back of *uke's* neck, locking his head and shoulders forward and down. *Tori's* right hip must pass distinctly further across *uke's* hips than in *tsurigoshi*.

Haraigoshi *(sweeping loin or hip)*

This is the first throw in this group in which *tori* raises one leg to act as a 'working' or throwing leg, while completely supporting his and his opponent's weight on the other leg – a throw in fact off one leg to the front. This is another very popular throw in competitions at all levels. It is most popular with tall people with long legs.

Haraigoshi departs from most of the other throws in Chapters 10 and 11 in that the working leg which is raised from the mat sweeps through the opponent's loin or upper thigh. Chest and body contact is vital for this throw to succeed and the strong lift-pull must be well co-ordinated with the footwork. The lift-pull itself differs from other throws. In nearly all the previous throws mentioned *tori* has to wrap his opponent's right arm down and across his stomach. If he does this in *haraigoshi, uke* can fend off because he will have been allowed to bend at the knees. *Tori* must therefore maintain a constant pull with his left hand up and past his own chin keeping his elbow high and thus stretching his opponent up the side of his body; he should aim at chest contact throughout own chest, rolling or shrugging the arm around his left shoulder and pulling *uke's* head towards his own.

Tori must not turn in too deep but should make contact all the way up his right side.

the action. If at the point of the throw *(kake)* the left foot is not turned sufficiently into the direction of the throw, *tori* will fall off balance himself.

This throw is one of the 'big guns' and once perfected is very difficult to counter or avoid. As with all throws, one should learn to use space effectively and fall into the direction of the throw. In completing the throw *tori* should not try to remain on balance himself but should lean into the right-front corner. Once the throw is completed *tori* can use his opponent's weight to check his own fall. If *tori* tries to execute the throw while remaining upright, *uke* can easily block him.

Tori's right leg has thus become the throwing leg and sweeps through *uke's* right loin,

Haraigoshi

Tori steps in with his lead right foot, landing almost between *uke's* feet. *Tori* should then replace his right foot with his left on the same spot, transferring his weight onto his left, which must be turned with the toes pointing towards *uke's* front. He should also achieve close chest and body contact by pulling *uke's* right arm up and past his

Alan Petherbridge, 6th Dan
Member of British European Championship Team 1957/8/9, individual European Champion 1961.

Haraigoshi

'I like the particular style of *haraigoshi* that I do because of the control one can maintain on the opponent's upper body once the technique is in motion. This way it has to score *ippon*.'

thereby knocking *uke's* legs from under him and backwards. *Tori* should continue the turn of his action, throwing his head around and down to his left.

Ukigoshi

Tori steps in to *uke* with his right foot and grips *uke* round the waist by driving his right arm between *uke's* left arm and trunk. He should not turn too deeply or bend his knees more than a little.

Tori must lock *uke* on to his own right hip.

Then with a powerful action, *tori* floats *uke* on to his right hip and wheels him over, gripping *uke*, powerfully with his right arm, which should extend round *uke's* waist as far as possible.

Ukigoshi *(floating hip)*

A successful *ukigoshi* depends much on footwork and also on *uke* stepping into a trap. To do this, *tori* must get *uke* to circle around him to his right and then release the right-hand grip and slip his arm around *uke's* waist. This throw should not be confused with *ogoshi* – the knees are not bent, nor are the hips raised.

Tsurikomigoshi

Tori steps in well across *uke* with his right foot and places it just in front of *uke's* right foot.

Keeping his feet fairly close together and his knees well bent, *tori* turns in deeply. His left foot must be between *uke's* feet, his right just in front of *uke's* right foot. *Tori* should not take his right elbow across

the front, but must keep it pinned, reinforcing its grip by driving it up into the left side of *uke's* trunk. *Tori* should pull all the time with his right hand—in fact he should try to pull his own right

thumb to his right ear. His hips must drive deep across *uke's* front. To throw, *tori* tucks forward and down,

at the same time straightening his legs and wrapping *uke's* right arm down across his chest and stomach.

As *uke* reaches the mat, *tori* wheels his head round to the left so that he is looking back to where *uke* was originally standing.

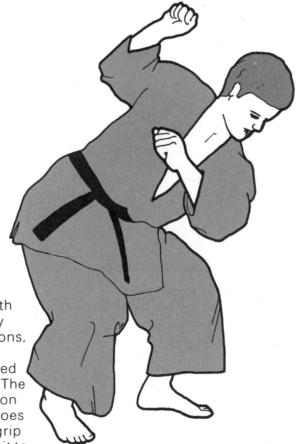

Tsurikomigoshi *(lift pull hip)*

This throw is very popular with small competitors and is very evident in grading competitions, where there are no weight categories and one is expected to fight all and varying sizes. The footwork and main body action is similar to *ogoshi,* but *tori* does not sacrifice his right-hand grip on *uke's* lapel, instead using it to rock his opponent's weight forward and on to the throw.

51

Sodetsurikomigoshi *(sleeve lift pull hip)*

This throw is not listed in the Gokyo because it is really a variation of *tsurikomigoshi.* It does however merit a mention and a place here since, because both hands grip at the opponent's lower sleeves, it can be easily attempted to both right and left without the warning of a changed grip being given.

Sodetsuri-komigoshi

This is a good throw for a competitor who likes to grip with both hands at his opponent's sleeves. In this case of *migi sodetsuri-komigoshi,* that is, a right sleeve lift-pull hip throw, *tori* should hold the underneath part of *uke's* left sleeve with his right hand well down. *Tori* steps across *uke's* front, his right foot landing just in front of *uke's* right foot.

He then spins his left foot back, leading with the heel, and plants it between *uke's* feet, at the same time driving his right hip across *uke* and forcing his left arm up. He must grip *uke's* jacket or the outer cuffs – contest rules are violated if he grips with even a single finger inside the sleeve.

To complete the throw, *tori* bends forward at the waist and straightens his legs, constantly driving the inside of his right arm against *uke's* left side and armpit. From the same grips one can practice this throw to the right and then to the left alternately. This is a good way to develop attacks on both sides.

Hanegoshi

Tori steps in with his right foot, quickly replacing this foot with his left, toes pointing towards *uke's* front, so that the right leg becomes the 'working' or 'throwing' leg. *Tori* should bend his right leg, keeping his knee well out to the side and brushing his instep against *uke's* right calf. *Tori* pulls *uke* to him, locking the entire length of *uke's* body to his own right side.

To develop the 'spring' action, *tori* twists his head to the left and down and straightens out his right, 'throwing' leg.

Hanegoshi (spring hip)

The entry for *hanegoshi* is the same as for *haraigoshi,* but the working leg should not straighten for a sweep but rather bends at the knee, *tori's* upper leg or thigh creating a kind of platform across *uke.* Just as with *haraigoshi, tori* should ensure that his support leg is bent initially so as to give a good spring action when it straightens for the throw and that his left foot is turned sufficiently and pointing into the direction of the throw.

Hanegoshi suits very well the short stocky type of build and is one of the classical judo throws, incorporating skill, grace, dynamic power and beauty.

To complete the throw with impetus, *tori* should strive to straighten his left supporting leg by coming up on to his toes, at the same time tucking his head down and round to the left.

Hanemakikomi

Stepping in with his right foot and transferring his weight quickly on to his left, which should be turned with the toes pointing to *uke's* front, *tori* turns his right leg into the 'working' or 'throwing' leg by bending it at the knee. The instep should touch *uke's* left leg just above the ankle.

At the same time *tori* releases his grip on *uke's* left lapel and circles his right arm up and over *uke's* head.

Driving his right arm up and forward in a big circle, *tori* straightens out his 'throwing' or right leg and twists his head down and round to his left.

Hanemakikomi *(winding spring hip)*

This is an extension or continuation of *hanegoshi* and like *sotomakikomi* should not be practised on the inexperienced.

He proceeds to 'wind' the whole action down into the mat and completes the throw. The extra drawing shows the point of *kake* from another angle, this is when *uke* has actually been lifted from the mat and is on his way over. *Tori* must lie into the direction of the throw and not remain upright.

Ushirogoshi

This counter-technique is best attempted against a throw to the front. *Uke* having attacked with *hanegoshi* or a similar throw, *tori* blocks him with his left hip, at the same time dropping his left hand down to *uke's* waist and circling it as far round as possible.

Ushirogoshi *(rear hip)*

This is a *kaeshiwaza* or counter-throw and is best attempted when *uke* has attempted a loin or hip technique.

To gain greater lift, some competitors lift and bend the left knee, using the left leg to help to lift *uke* high into the air. In this way, *uke's* legs are swept up, and he is upended completely.

Tori must also drop his own bodyweight and bend slightly at the knees, ensuring, however, that he is not pulled forward. Gripping his opponent securely round the middle, *tori* lifts him up, arching his body by thrusting his hips forward and thrusting the upper part of his body backwards.

At the peak of the lift he swings his opponent up feet first and releases his left arm from around *uke's* waist. By arching and driving his hips up at the correct second, *tori* can lift his opponent high into the air for the perfect counter-technique.

Utsurigoshi *(changing hip)*

This impressive technique is a useful counter-action against any of the loin or hip techniques. It depends on a great deal of skill and good timing and an instinctive sense of when the opponent is about to attack.

The first part is exactly the same as **ushirogoshi,** but on bouncing **uke** up into the air with the front part of his left hip **tori** then swings his left hip across while **uke** is in the air and catches him on the side of his left hip as **uke** descends. At the same time **tori** seizes **uki's** body around the waist and then throws **uke** with what is now in effect a left **ogoshi.**

Although at first sight this seems impossibly difficult, it has a high scoring rate among counter-techniques in major competition. But, as with all counter-techniques, it depends on the force of the opponent's first attack and on the skill and timing of **tori.**

A player should never depend entirely upon counter-techniques, nor should he get into the bad habit of waiting for the opportunity to do one. Many a contest has been lost in this way, and of course if a player only waits for a counter-opportunity the referee will penalize him under the 'passivity' ruling – and that can mean complete disqualification from a competition.

Utsurigoshi

This is a counter-technique for use when **tori** has been able to anticipate his opponent's attack. Dropping his hips by bending slightly at the knees, **tori** secures **uke's** middle by dropping his left hand and encircling **uke's** waist. Arching backwards with a powerful lift **tori** bounces **uke** up with his left hip. He then swings his left hip through so that **uke** lands across his back. Bending now at the middle **tori** dips forward, throwing his own head round to the right, and rolls **uke** over his own back. With a strong right-hand pull with his right elbow pressing into his own right groin, **tori** throws **uke** cleanly on to his back.

CHAPTER 12. ASHIWAZA – FOOT AND LEG TECHNIQUES

This is a group of reaping throws which succeed by the sweeping or swinging action of a working or throwing leg. Many of them are to the rear, in effect throwing *uke* backwards.

Ouchigari *(major inner reaping)*
Ouchigari is a 'light throw', without the overall power of a 'big gun'. Nevertheless, this and throws like it are an essential part of the repertoire of a good contest man. Even if they do not always work, they are ideal for getting an attack going and opening up the defence of a difficult opponent.

The basic aim is to get the opponent's weight over on to one leg and then to sweep or reap away that leg. But the action is not that simple and all the movements of the body must be co-ordinated.

To start with, there must be a powerful drive off the back and supporting foot. To do this, *tori* places his left foot centrally on the mat. Just as a boxer is taught to punch his weight off the back foot, so a judo competitor is taught to drive his weight off the back foot into the throwing action. At the same time *tori* swings his right leg across the front of *uke* and then back and through *uke's* legs, heel first, to sweep or strike *uke's* left leg just below and behind the knee. The upper drive or push should not be with straight arms for this would keep *uke* at bay and help him to keep away from the reaping leg, but with bent arms and directed towards *uke's* left rear quarter. If the push is allowed to change direction towards his right rear he will be able to place all his weight safely on the foot that *tori* is not attacking and lift his other leg out of danger.

Remember to keep low by bending at the knees while attacking with any of these throws to the rear. *Uke's* natural defence will force *tori* to 'ride up' as he thrusts forward and if he rides up too high *uke* can easily counter him. *Tori's* 'power curve', created by arching his back with hips thrusting forward, is important. He should also make sure that his upper weight lies forward into the drive.

A difficult and defensive opponent will attempt to hop out of the danger of the reaping foot – some are quite good at this. In such a situation *tori* should be prepared to follow up his attack by hopping forward and off the back foot as often as necessary to bring *uke* down on to his back. Even is he is knocked down, a crafty opponent can frustrate *tori's* attempts to score maximum points by sitting down on the throw. If this happens, *tori* should be prepared to follow through by running round or over *uke's* legs to pin *uke's* shoulders firmly on the mat. In fact the mark of a good competitor is to make absolutely sure of the maximum score by following through into a hold.

At the same time he should drive his upper weight forward, laying into *uke's* left chest with bent right arm. If *tori* straightens his right arm too early, he will push *uke* back and in fact help him to avoid the throw.

Ouchigari
Tori brings his left foot to a central position for the drive-off. He hops on that foot and hooks his right foot through and between *uke's* legs to catch *uke's* lower calf and sweeps or reaps, with heel leading, out to the side and back towards his own position.

The drive should be continued down to the mat, following through to ensure that *uke's* shoulders go right back to the mat. *Tori* should be prepared to hop on his support foot a number of times in order to press home the attack.

Osotogari

Stepping in with his left foot so that it is almost in line with *uke's* feet, *tori* slips

uke's right arm defence round his left upper arm with his left hand. Planting his weight firmly on his left

foot, he swings his right leg through and between his own left leg and *uke's* right leg.

His right-hand holds high at *uke's* left lapel.

Striking *uke* high behind the right thigh, *tori* reaps back with his working right leg in a big powerful arc, driving his head down into the mat and forming a 'T' shape with his body.

He hugs *uke's* head to him, his overall lift-pull and bodyweight bringing *uke* right over so that all *uke's* weight goes onto the heel of his right foot, which will soon be swept away.

Osotogari *(major outer reaping)*

This is a big 'power' throw to the rear and one that is easy for beginners to understand. The principle is to get *uke* over on to one leg by coming in alongside him and hugging his upper weight to one's own chest, swinging the working leg past *uke* on the outside of his leg and then back to strike *uke* high behind his thigh, so downing him backwards with a powerful sweep.

Tori should not let himself be forced back off balance while performing the action, for if there is anything wrong with his technique and he himself is off balance he can easily be

countered with another *osotogari.* So be careful, keep the upper weight thrusting forward into the action and keep low by bending the support leg at the beginning. This leg should straighten out when the other, working, leg is sweeping back and actually throwing the opponent. In unbalancing his opponent, *tori* should ensure that his opponent's head is forced or rocked over on to the leg that is going to be swept away. Otherwise, at the crucial moment, *uke* can easily frustrate the throw by leaning his head over to his left shoulder, so transferring all his weight over

on to the leg that is not being attacked.

In completing the throw, *tori* should form a 'T' shape with his body, driving his own head down into the mat towards the spot where he intends to throw his opponent. The toes of the sweeping leg should be pointed to keep the leg straight and the muscle formation at the back of the thigh taut and hardened for the impact of the reap.

This throw is very popular among big men and can be used against an opponent of similar height and size. It should not be attempted by a small man on a much bigger opponent.

Tony Sweeney, 5th Dan
British International many times,
National Coach.

Hizaguruma
'I like *hizaguruma* because it is a
technique which can work very
well against an opponent with a
defensive posture. I have also
found *hizaguruma* useful
because it is a throw which
combines with major throws
when used on the opposite side
to such a major throw. It works
particularly well when a sleeve
grip at the elbow is employed and
the stiffening defensive actions
of the opponent are in fact an
advantage – thus left *osotogari* –
right *hizaguruma*.'

Hizaguruma
This throw is very
similar to
sasaetsurikomiashi,
except that *tori*
wheels his
opponent round
himself and catches
the outside of *uke's*
right knee. His

working foot should
not catch the front
of *uke's* knee or
kneecap. Care
should be taken not
to catch *uke's* knee

too early in the
throw. With the aid
of his right arm, *tori*
should push *uke's*
left arm up and
drive in the circular
direction in which
his left hand is

pulling. *Tori* should
continue wheeling,
using his body-
weight to draw
uke over his right
front, at the crucial
moment catching
uke's knee on the
outside by using his
left foot like a cat's
paw, making
contact with the
sole of the foot.

Sasaetsurikomiashi *(propping drawing ankle)*

This is the first throw in which the foot actually has to touch the opponent. There is no distinction between foot and leg in the Japanese language, *ashi* meaning foot *or* leg. There is no actual sweeping action in this throw, which probably makes it the best *ashiwaza* to start people off with. Beginners tend to hack or kick when attempting a sweep. The best opportunity for it is when *uke* is stepping forward.

Sasaetsurikomiashi

This propping and drawing ankle throw is achieved by *tori* lifting *uke* forward on to his toes. *Tori* pulls *uke's* right elbow up and out to his right-front corner and with his right hand applies a lift-pull on *uke's* left lapel. He must step in but at the same time keep his head and shoulders back, using his bodyweight to draw *uke* forward.

He places his left foot on *uke's* instep, endeavouring to keep a straight line from head to the toes of the left foot, which acts as the working foot.

Tori does not sweep with the left foot but rather uses it as a propping foot while, with bodyweight and arms, wheeling *uke* over it to throw *uke* into *uke's* own right front space.

Haraitsurikomiashi

At the exact moment when **uke** steps back on to his right foot and is about to put his weight on it, **tori** catches **uke's** right instep with the bottom of his sweeping foot, sweeping it further back from the spot where **uke** had originally intended to step.

Haraitsurikomiashi *(sweeping drawing ankle)*

This throw is like **sasaetsurikomiashi** but is better used when **uke** is stepping backwards.

Pulling with the left hand at **uke's** right elbow and driving up and across **uke's** upper chest with the right hand, **tori** draws **uke's** upper weight over **tori's** sweeping foot and throws him in a big circular action.

As with *sasaetsurikomiashi*, **tori** should maintain a straight line from the head through the body to the toes of the sweeping leg.

61

Deashiharai *(foot sweep)*
Foot throws depend on pure timing and skill. Very little effort is needed for this one. Success depends on *tori* catching his opponent just as the foot to be attacked is about to settle on the mat after a forward step.

Deashiharai
As *uke* advances his right foot, *tori* catches it on the outside with the bottom of his left foot and sweeps across at the exact moment that *uke* places his weight forward on to his right foot. *Tori's* left arm bears down, the heel of the hand at *uke's* right elbow; simultaneously his right arm drives up and through *uke's* chin in a tight, powerful circle.

Tori should not break or bend in the middle as he completes the sweep and should sweep as far as possible, the outside edge of his left foot brushing the surface of the mat in a straight line across his front.

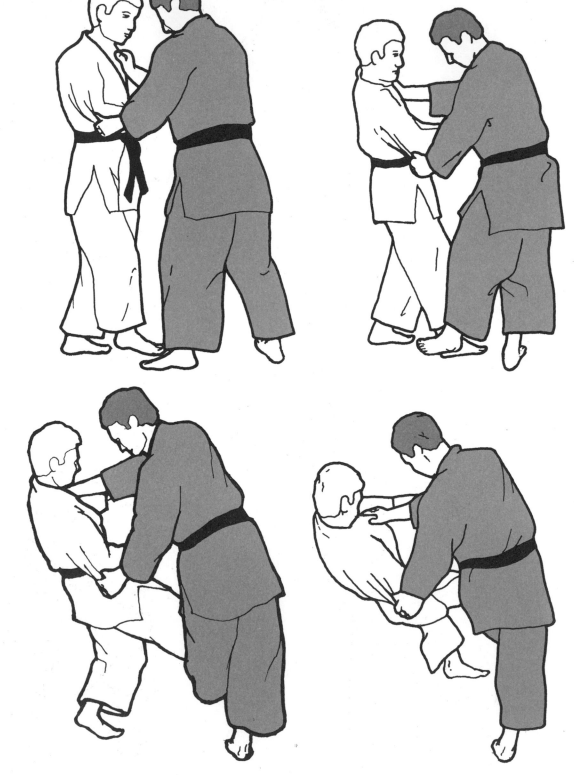

Kouchigari *(minor inner reaping)*
This throw is best achieved as the end result of a combination movement. The hand action differs from the other throws in that *tori* hangs his weight on *uke's* left lapel and right sleeve at the elbow.

Danny DaCosta, 3rd Dan
British Open Champion several times, European silver medallist 1974, British international several times.
Kouchigari
'I like *kouchigari,* particularly on the left, because it is a good opener and has bags of commitment. Sometimes it can be used with both hands on the one side. It is a good opener for other throws and is particularly good for following through into groundwork.'

Kouchigari
Tori places his left foot in a central drive-off position. He then bears his weight down on *uke* so as to get a response and with his right foot sweeps in between *uke's* feet, catching *uke's* right heel with the bottom of his foot.

Attempting to drive with his right fore-arm through the centre of *uke's* chest, *tori* drives his upper bodyweight into the action, sweeping towards his own left foot with a straight leg and driving his right hip forward. *Tori* should not bend at the waist while attempting this throw.

When the sweep becomes effective *tori* should try to pin *uke's* right elbow into *uke's* stomach so that he is unable to use this arm to defend and maintain his balance.

63

Uchimata *(inner thigh)*
Uchimata is one of the few throws in this group in which *uke* is thrown to his front and not backwards. As a contest throw it has no equal in weight category contests. Generally, it is inadvisable for a small man to attempt this throw on a bigger opponent – but then there is always the odd exception, one of the delightful surprises in judo competition.

As with most of the big throws, *uchimata* has a number of variations and styles which individuals have developed as part of their particular make-up. There are two main styles however: *ouchimata,* the deep turn, and *kouchimata,* the straight leg sweep. In *ouchimata, tori* hops in and turns to land supported on his left foot, the working leg sweeping the inside of the thigh of *uke's* leg. *Tori* should ensure that he is locking *uke's* upper body forward and down. If this is done correctly, *uke* will be tipped forward with

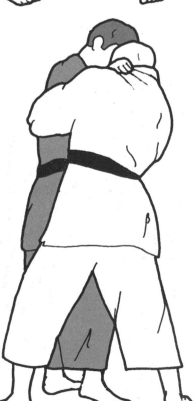

Uchimata
Tori prepares to hop in on his left foot by stepping with his right foot to a point between *uke's* feet. He then hops in on his left foot, making sure that its toes point to *uke's* front and in the direction of the throw. If his foot is not turned sufficiently, *tori* will collapse when he takes all the weight of both himself and his opponent on his left leg.

The right leg now becomes the throwing leg and sweeps up between *uke's* legs.
At the same time *tori* should pull *uke* forward, bringing *uke's* head,

his right shoulder dipping down towards the mat and *tori's* working leg will sweep up, striking high inside *uke's* upper thigh. In *ouchimata,* contact is made by *tori* with the back of his thigh, in *kouchimata* with the outside of the thigh. To get a powerful sweep in *kouchimata,* the working leg should be kept

as straight as possible, with the toes pointed.

In completing the throw *tori* should turn his head to his left. He must NOT, repeat NOT, tuck his head under, so that the top of his head touches the mat. A number of serious accidents, some fatal, have been caused when the throw has broken his spinal cord because he took his head straight down to the mat.

Brian Jacks, 6th Dan
Olympic bronze medallist, four times European Champion, British Open Champion several times.

Uchimata

'I personally do *uchimata* more so than other throws mainly because I believe it's the most beautiful looking throw in judo. If you look at gymnasts or ballet dancers and such like, you can see the beauty of their movement. Something like this is present in *uchimata,* which takes full commitment from the beginning of the throw to the end. One can see the extended leg, the pointed toe and indeed the whole beauty of overall bodily action. As a throw that wins contests, *uchimata* has got all the attributes that one needs for making a full *ippon* score. Certainly this has been the case for me personally — if one works hard enough on it, it is guaranteed to score 95 per cent of the time.'

shoulders and chest down towards the mat. *Tori* should continue his right leg sweep as far and as high as possible, turning his head to the left at the end of the throw. To get

maximum impetus *tori* should lift by driving his left supporting leg straight and by stretching up on the toes of his left foot.

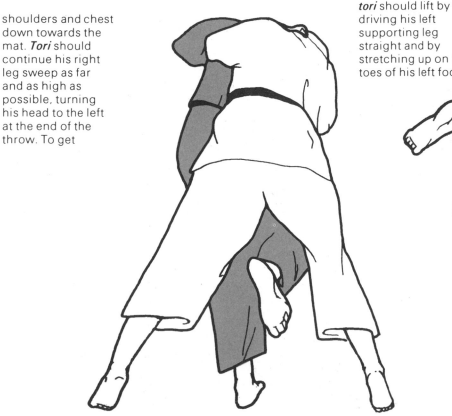

Kouchigake *(minor inner hook)*
This throw is ideal for a small man confronting a long-legged opponent. Juniors of an early age also like it.

In following through, *tori* should ensure that he himself is not trapped in groundwork, if his efforts have not already given him the maximum score. Should he turn his head to look back, he could easily be strangled as a result of exposing his neck. He should look into the mat throughout the action and keep his chin firmly tucked in to his own upper chest.

Kouchigake
Gripping *uke's* sleeve with his left hand, *tori* drives his right arm straight between *uke's* right arm and waist. At the same time, driving off his back foot, he hooks his right leg low through and between *uke's* legs to hook around *uke's* right leg.

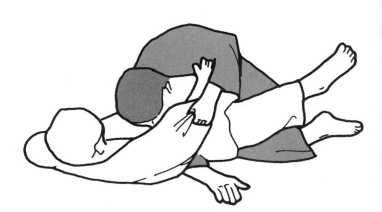

Gripping this leg tight with his right leg, *tori* should drive the back of his right shoulder into *uke's* middle, pushing off his back (left) foot all the time.

At this point he should be prepared to hop forward as many times as necessary to force *uke* down on to his back and to follow through into *kouchigakemakikomi.* The power-drive off the back foot is essential if this technique is to be successful.

Kosotogari

Tori steps in towards *uke*, his left foot landing almost level with the outside of *uke's* right foot. He then quickly transfers his weight, bringing his right foot forward *(tsugi ashi)* and catches *uke's* heel with the bottom of his left foot. At the same time he presses down, still

Kosotogari *(minor outside reap)*

Stepping forward with his leading left foot close to *uke's* right foot and forcing *uke* back to his right-rear corner and over on to his right heel, *tori* brings up his back right foot for greater support and lifts his left foot to catch the back of *uke's* right heel. Again the reaping action is made with the bottom of *tori's* foot reaping toward the direction in which *tori* was originally standing.

holding *uke's* right sleeve with the heel of his hand and tries to pin *uke's* right elbow into *uke's* side or even as far as his stomach. Still

holding *uke's* left lapel with his right hand, he should at the same time drive directly through *uke's* chin from the front.

Using his left foot as his working foot, *tori* should sweep *uke's* right foot forward in the direction of the toes of *uke's* right foot.

Nidankosotogari *(double minor outside reap)*

This throw is an extension or continuation technique *(renzokuwaza)* of *kosotogari* used when the opponent has avoided *kosotogari* by lifting his left foot forward and out of trouble. In so doing, *uke* has to place all his weight on to his other foot. However he is still driven backwards with the upper drive derived from *tori's* efforts, and so his weight is rocking back onto his left heel. Tori transfers his attack with his working leg to the furthest heel. The subtle timing needed for this throw can result in *uke* being upended with considerable force.

Nidankosotogari

If, after *tori* has attacked *uke* with *kosotogake, uke* lifts his right foot out of the way of *tori's* left, *tori* can then reach round with his left foot and trap the heel of *uke's* right foot. *Uke* is now completely balanced on his left foot, and *tori* can sweep him to the ground.

Kosotogake *(minor outside hook)*

This throw is very similar to *kosotogari* and could in fact be said to be just a variation. The difference is in the action of the working leg. In this case the working foot goes further around behind *uke's* lower right leg and hooks round it. *Tori* must commit his upper bodyweight more into this throw and drive *uke* backwards into *uke's* right rear corner, so making up for the lack of reaping or sweeping back action that was the main feature in *kosotogari*.

Nidankosotogake *(double minor outside hook)*

This throw serves *kosotogake* just as *nidankosotogari* does for *kosotogari*.
With all four of the *kosoto* throws, *tori* should make sure that he does not fall past *uke* or slip round behind him when attempting the throw. If he does so he will lose the power to finish the throw and will probably fall to the mat himself. Neither *nidankosotogake* nor *nidankosotogari* are mentioned in the Gokyo, but they are very common now in judo practise. and competition.

Kosotogake

Just as in *kosoto-gari, tori* steps in towards *uke*, bringing his left foot almost level with *uke's* right.

Tori then quickly changes the position of his feet, bringing his right foot up to the same spot and hooking his left leg round *uke's* right leg just below and behind the knee.

At the same time he should pin *uke's* right elbow into *uke's* side and try to drive it even deeper across *uke's* stomach.

The right hand should hold *uke's* jacket at the left lapel and at the same time drive through *uke's* chin from the front. In hooking with the left throwing, leg, *tori* should try to lift that leg and at the same time force *uke* backwards with his right fore-arm into the throw.

Oguruma

Spinning on the ball of his right foot, *tori* should sweep his left leg round in a semi-circle, heel leading, landing close to his right foot. In so doing he must also drive through *uke's* chest with his right hand still holding *uke's* left lapel and pull *uke's* right elbow up and out into *uke's* right front corner, keeping his left hand at *uke's* right sleeve.

Tori should then place his right leg across the front of *uke* with the heel slightly above and past *uke's* right knee.
Using this leg as a bar, he should wheel *uke* over his right leg, tipping *uke's* head and shoulders forward. *Uke* should feel as if he is being tipped forward over a low wall without being able to step forward to regain his balance.

Oguruma *(major wheel)*

In *oguruma, tori* turns into *uke* by spinning on his right foot, and sweeping his left foot in a circle with heel leading, planting it in front of *uke's* left foot. Placing his weight completely on his left foot, *tori* raises his right leg straight and places the back of his right heel just above and on the outside edge of *uke's* right knee. With a powerful action of the shoulders and trunk similar to that needed for *taiotoshi, tori* wheels his opponent over his outstretched leg. The raised right leg does not sweep, but rather acts as a bar or low barrier over which *tori* overturns his opponent.

Ashiguruma

With his right foot brought to a central position from which to spin, *tori* swings his left foot back in a semi-circle to land just on the outside of *uke's* left foot. Placing all his weight on his left foot, *tori* sweeps the back of his right leg across the shin of *uke's* right leg. *Uke* must at the same time be brought forward on to his toes and his upper weight wheeled over *tori's* right leg, which should be sweeping or reaping back. *Uke* should be stretched at the point of the sweep, so that he cannot bend in the middle and frustrate the throw.

Ashiguruma *(leg wheel)*

The entry for this is the same as in *oguruma,* but *tori's* working leg catches *uke's* right leg lower down, just above the ankle on the lower shin. *Uke* is wheeled over *tori's* working leg, which can also sweep back to assist the throw.

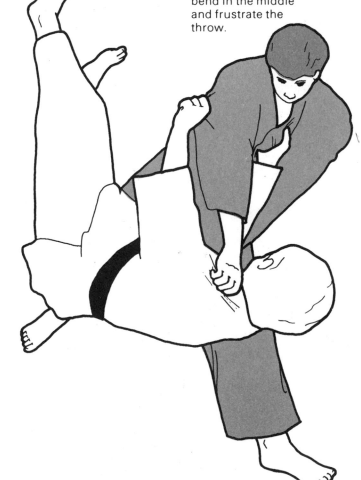

Okuriashiharai

This foot sweep is best achieved when both competitors are moving to the side (in this case *tori* is moving to his right).

As *uke* moves his right foot towards his left foot, *tori* should catch the outside of *uke's* right foot with the bottom of his left foot.

He sweeps *uke's* right foot further than *uke* had intended to step. *Tori* must catch and sweep *uke's* right foot at the crucial moment. *Tori* should then

Okuriashiharai *(side sweeping ankle throw)*

This throw is perhaps the most impressive of the *ashiwaza* series, but it does take time to perfect. The best opportunity is when the opponent is moving sideways. *Okuriashiharai* is ideal in a fast-moving contest but really requires split-second timing.

sweep with a straight leg, endeavouring to sweep *uke* cleanly off both his feet. As *tori's* left foot follows through the sweep, *tori* should pull *uke's* elbow sharply to his left side. This should prevent his upper weight following his feet and thus bringing him completely off balance.

Kanibasami

A good opening for this throw is when *tori* has been able to position himself alongside *uke* or because of *uke's* defence from another move, has found himself alongside *uke*. Keeping hold of *uke's* left lapel with his right hand, *tori* places his left hand as close as possible to *uke's* left foot. Bearing all his weight on the palm of his left hand, *tori* swings his legs

straight, bringing his right leg up high in front of *uke* so that he touches *uke's* chest with his calf and his left leg behind *uke* so that his instep touches *uke's* right heel. *Tori* should swing his legs into the action as straight as possible, crashing his right leg into *uke's* chest and placing his left foot so that *uke* cannot step back and regain his balance. With his legs wide apart, *tori* twists from the waist in order to knock *uke* backwards. *Tori* should then follow through into groundwork.

Kanibasami *(scissors)*

Kanibasami, sometimes known as *kanihasami,* is not included in the Gokyo but is a popular move for the more experienced. It is a very good technique to use against an opponent who has a rigid, strong-arm defence and also when all else fails.

In doing the 'scissor' action with the legs, *tori* should keep his feet wide apart. If they are close together he will lack leverage with which to force *uke* backwards.

Osotoguruma *(major outer wheel)*

Osotoguruma is much the same as *osotogari*, the difference being that *tori* sweeps away both legs rather than the nearest one. The fall from this throw is very heavy indeed. The success rate is very low on the scoring charts as an experienced person just would not allow his opponent to get sufficiently far around his back in order to sweep both legs.

Osotoguruma

Stepping in alongside *uke* with his left foot, *tori* brings *uke* over on to the heel of *uke's* right leg (as with *osotogari*) and swings his right leg through between his left leg and *uke's* right leg.

He then stretches his right throwing leg across the back of *uke's* legs and with a powerful left-hand pull across his own stomach locks *uke's* upper-right chest to his own chest and wheels his opponent over his right out-stretched leg. *Tori* must not step too deep initially with his left foot, since he is then not bearing all his own weight and that of *uke's* back over on to *uke's* right heel and may easily be countered.

Yoko-otoshi *(side drop)*

This is a sacrifice throw: that is, *tori* sacrifices his own body position by going down on his back or side onto the mat in order to throw.

Yoko-otoshi

The attack is usually made when *uke* is moving to the side. As *uke* moves to his right and is just about to place his weight on his right foot, *tori* should step in.

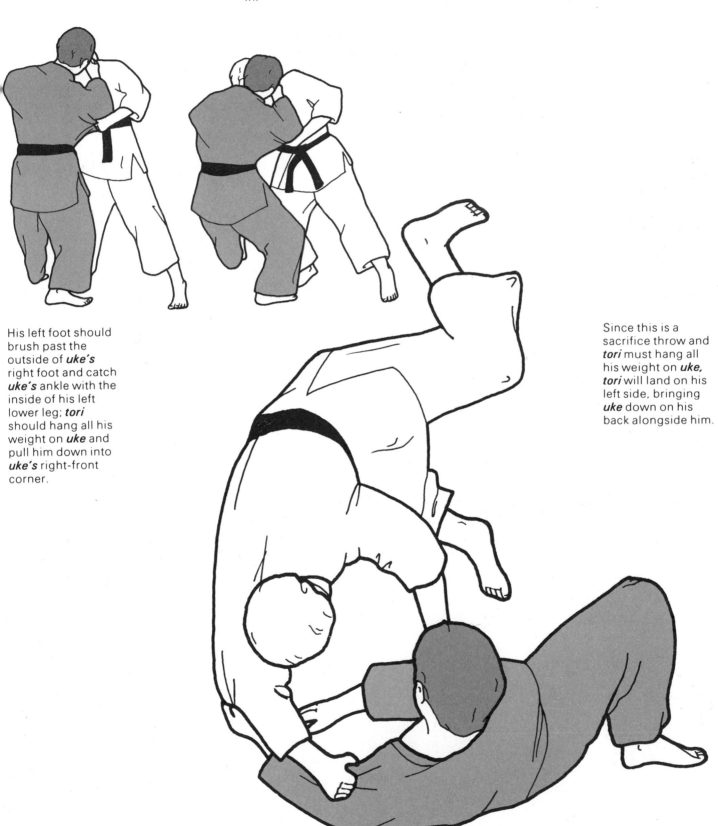

His left foot should brush past the outside of *uke's* right foot and catch *uke's* ankle with the inside of his left lower leg; *tori* should hang all his weight on *uke* and pull him down into *uke's* right-front corner.

Since this is a sacrifice throw and *tori* must hang all his weight on *uke*, *tori* will land on his left side, bringing *uke* down on his back alongside him.

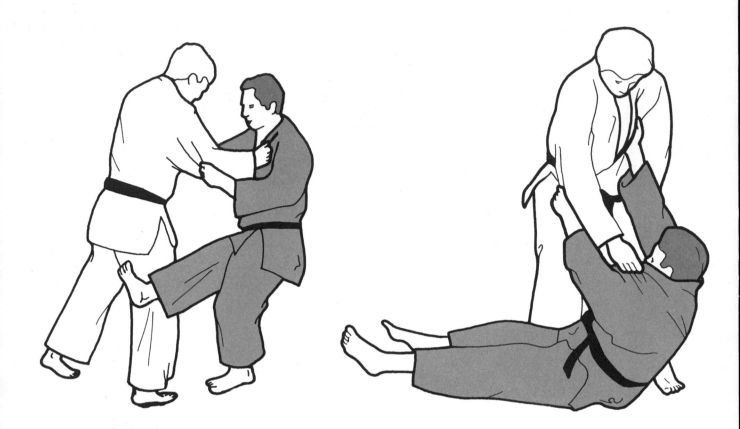

Yokowakare

This sacrifice throw depends upon *tori* using his entire bodyweight to dash his opponent to the floor. Throwing his right leg across the front of *uke* to land straight with the heel just on the outside of *uke's* right foot, *tori* goes down to the mat, landing along his left side and wheeling *uke* over the top of his own prostrate body. *Tori* should continue turning to his left to complete the throw and should roll up on to his own feet or be prepared to follow through with a hold.

Tomoenage *(stomach throw)*

The stomach or 'high circle' throw is one of the most impressive in this group and is a popular contest throw.

Tomoenage

As this is a sacrifice throw, it has to work; there is otherwise a danger of getting caught in groundwork and held down while attempting it.

Tori should drive his left leg straight between *uke's* legs and at the same time hop into the air, bending his right, throwing, leg as much as

possible. The right foot should make contact just underneath *uke's* belt knot. To bring *uke* forward on to the throw *tori* must suspend his body-weight, bending his arms. In dropping under his opponent, *tori* should aim to land with his

buttocks between *uke's* feet. If he does not sit under sufficiently, *uke* will be able to brace against the throw.

When *tori* is on his back he completes the throw by straightening his right leg sharply, but not too early.

In order to achieve maximum score, he should continue to hold *uke's* jacket with one hand (in this case the left). This ensures that *uke* will be flipped over and will be unable to walk out of trouble on his hands or do a 'butterfly twist'.

Sumigaeshi

This is another sacrifice throw rather like **tomoenage** and is best used on a very defensive opponent who has bent forward. It can also be attempted from high holds behind the opponent's neck or even with one hand gripping the opponent's back down to the belt. In this case **tori** crouches and sweeps his throwing (right) leg, so that his instep makes contact inside **uke's** left thigh.

Sumigaeshi *(corner throw)*

This throw is best attempted when the opponent is on the defensive and bending forward with feet well apart and knees bent.

Tori should wheel his opponent over the top by dropping to the mat on his back and using the full weight of his body to tip *uke* forward.

To complete the throw *tori* straightens his right leg. This must be at the correct moment, not too early.

Taniotoshi *(valley drop)*

In a deep wrestling-style grip, *tori* throws his left leg round behind *uke* and plants his left foot on the mat just behind *uke's* left foot. *Tori* then falls away into *uke's* right rear corner, taking *uke* with him.

Taniotoshi

This valley drop is very much the same as *yoko-otoshi,* except that *tori* slides his left leg as far as he can past the outside of *uke's* right foot and drives *uke's* weight back into *uke's* right-rear corner.

In sliding his leading leg well past *uke, tori* must also slide all his bodyweight under and past *uke,* literally hanging on him so that *uke* falls backwards. *Tori's* right hand can grip *uke's* left lapel or slip under *uke's* left armpit to drive him backward.

The throw is completed with *tori* on his back wheeling *uke* over his outstretched left leg.

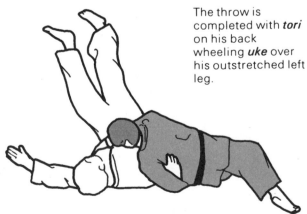

79

Ukiwaza

This sacrifice throw depends largely upon *tori* catching his opponent off balance at *uke's* right front corner. Throwing his left leg well out to his left, *tori* hangs all his weight on *uke*.

Ukiwaza *(floating throw)*

This throw is rarely seen in contest these days and is very difficult to do against an experienced opponent.

This forces *tori* to tip forward to *uke's* right front corner. *Tori* should throw his left leg out straight so as to add further weight.

Tori literally hangs all his weight on *uke,* forcing him down and whirling him over the top in a circular action. *Tori* must throw *uke* clear of his own body by pulling sharply at *uke's* right elbow at the end of the throw.

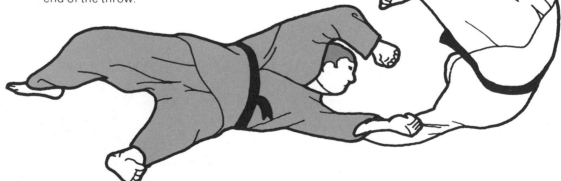

Yokoguruma *(side wheel)*
Yokoguruma is very effective as a counter to most throws to the front.

Yokoguruma
The side wheel is a counter/continuation technique. *Uke* has attacked with a throw to the front such as *ogoshi* or *hanegoshi* and *tori* intends to counter with a throw such as *utsurigoshi*. *Uke* has in turn seen the trap and has dropped his weight so as to frustrate the lift for *utsurigoshi*. With his left arm locking around *uke's* waist, *tori* lifts his right foot.

In one movement he swings his right leg in a big arc round to *uke's* front, through and between *uke's* legs. *Tori's* bodyweight should follow the weight of his right leg so that he sits down between *uke's* feet on his right buttock.

He then wheels *uke* over his left shoulder.

81

Uranage *(rear throw)*
This throw is like *yokoguruma,* in that *tori* uses it as a counter-technique. The fall from this throw is very heavy and should never be attempted on the inexperienced.

Uranage

This is used either as a counter-technique or as a direct throw. *Tori* should bend at the knees and seize *uke* round the waist with his left arm.

He places the heel of his right hand at *uke's* abdomen. Lifting *uke* high into the air and himself arching backwards, *tori* falls backwards, taking his opponent with him. Before he lands on his back, *tori* throws *uke* clear over his left shoulder, making sure that he releases his left arm before they both land on the mat.

Tori's right arm should continue to drive *uke* over his left shoulder right to the end.

Yokogake *(side drop)*
This throw develops out of *sasaetsurikomiashi.* The fall is very sharp, and a swift, effective breakfall is necessary.

Yokogake

As *uke* advances with his right foot, *tori* steps in with his right foot to a point in line with *uke's* toes and his right leg slightly bent with hips well forward. At the same time, gripping *uke's* left lapel with his right hand, he lifts under *uke,* assisted by the force of his forearm driving up. His left hand pulls *uke's* right arm up and out to *uke's* right-front corner.

When *tori* has extended *uke* on to the toes of *uke's* right foot, he should sweep with the sole of his left foot through *uke's* instep, hanging his weight and falling back himself like a log. *Tori* should not bend at the middle as he falls backwards. He should land on his left side, *uke* landing alongside him on his back.

Sukuinage
As *uke* steps in to attack *tori* with a major body throw such as *haraigoshi tori* lowers his hips and prepares to move in behind *uke* and under his centre of gravity.

Before *uke's* throw can gather momentum, *tori* brings his hips into a position squarely behind and slightly below *uke's* buttocks, at the same time driving his left arm across the front of *uke's* body and down past *uke's* left thigh.

Tori thrusts upward with his hips and, as the weight comes off *uke's* feet, scoops *uke's* legs up with his hands so that *uke's* upper body drops backward like a stone to the mat.

CHAPTER 14. COMBINATION AND CONTINUATION TECHNIQUES

This book covers most of the single techniques used in judo. There are however numerous variations and adaptions derived from these techniques.

As an individual's judo improves, it soon becomes apparent that the 'single' technique no longer brings the same results. Better and stronger opposition is met, and as the individual's style and technique become familiar it is increasingly difficult to score with the 'single' attempt. So it is necessary to develop methods designed to lure an opponent into a throw (though the possibility of the single throw should never be completely discarded). This is usually after about a year of hard and regular training.

A simple example of a combination technique is when *tori* attacks with a 'single' throw designed to throw *uke* in a certain direction and *uke* blocks the throw or defends against it so as to leave *tori* vulnerable to an attack in another direction, usually the opposite of that of the first throw. This is merely a basic example; in time a player will extend the range and direction of combinations. This is one of the most fascinating aspects of advanced judo.

Let us take one set of simple opposite direction combinations and see how they work, in this case based on a throw to the front off two feet such as *taiotoshi* or *morote seoinage*. *Uke* either has the experience to see the throw coming or *tori's* attempted throw has not been strong enough. *Uke* is now defending strongly against the threat to his front; this leaves him weak at his rear. At precisely the right moment (this is important – not too early and not too late), *tori* changes the direction of his attack and attempts *ouchigari* (or *kouchigari*). Because *uke* is momentarily weak to his rear, he will therefore be thrown with the second attempt. The same combination can be applied the

other way round. *Tori* attacks with *ouchigari, uke* defends by running back and keeping his legs away from the danger of the *gari* but momentarily leaves himself weak to a throw to the front such as *taiotoshi;* and so *tori* does just that – he changes direction and throws with *taiotoshi.*

Combinations are also a good deterrent to counter-techniques. By keeping constantly on the move and attacking in different directions, a contestant is less prone to a counter-attack. Counter-attacks are only possible when the contestant's attack has fizzled out and he is momentarily 'frozen' and therefore vulnerable.

Usually a player builds his combination on his best single throw, one that he has developed a little more than others. But the final result can often depend on the weaker of the two throws used in the combination. In that case the strength and powerful threat of the first technique will have left the opponent 'wide open' to the second, weaker, technique.

The first technique in a combination is often described as a 'feint', though this is inaccurate. In boxing a contestant must respect a feint and take necessary precautions by maintaining his guard or reacting with a counter-punch. Not so in judo. An experienced *judoka* will not react unless he feels that the first attack is a genuine effort. He has learned to 'feel' the quality of an attack through his arms and his grip on his opponent – not by what he sees. Remember therefore that the first attack in a combination must be full-blooded and have every intention of throwing the opponent. Only when his attack has been stopped and it is impossible to continue in the direction originally intended should *tori* change to the second throw of the combination. And of course not all combinations are 'doubles'; the more advanced *judoka* will continue

his attacks from one direction to another, then to another and yet another until he has achieved some kind of success. For this a player must be very fit indeed and have sufficient stamina to maintain and pursue the attacks.

The advanced competitor must also be adept in continuation attack. A continuation attack simply involves continuing with a second or third attack but using the same throw, adapting it a little or changing direction. Sometimes a contestant who has successfully stopped a throw feels safe in the knowledge that his opponent will not attack again with the same throw within the next few seconds and therefore relaxes his defence against it – that is the moment when a 'double attack' can pay dividends.

Osotogari can be used as an example. *Tori* attacks with *osotogari,* but *uke* has had sufficient time to defend. *Tori* presses home the attack by hopping forward in short hops on the supporting foot and changing his big backwards reap with a throwing leg into a hook. This change of tactic, which continues the attack in the same direction, has won many a contest. Even if *uke* has still been able to withstand this continuation attack, *tori* has the opportunity to turn it into a combination by planting his throwing leg on the mat between *uke's* feet and swinging the other foot round behind to catch *uke's* furthest foot for *nidankosotogari.* There is no end to the possibilities.

Work on a throw, build it up until it becomes a match 'winner', then work on methods to enhance that throw yet more and add little tricks with which to continue the attacks; then find a throw that will complement your original throw, and make up a combination. When you have developed that combination try it the opposite way round. Search and experiment continuously and in doing so analyze the movements and reactions of your opponents.

If combinations and continuations add a whole new dimension to *tachiwaza* (standing judo), the range and possibilities in groundwork are yet greater. In groundwork one should be prepared to move from one attempt to another depending on the opponent's reaction. Many opportunities are missed for combination attacks on the mat: just as an attempt at a strangle is about to succeed, many attackers give up and move to another technique. A player must be fluent in groundwork, and prepare his moves well in advance so that he can plan ahead and goad or lead his opponent step by step into the final trap. And in getting him there the really clever groundwork exponent will make his opponent do all the work and eventually exhaust himself, so making the grand finale that much easier.

Groundwork

The main point in groundwork or grappling techniques is to immobilize the opponent by holding him firmly on his back or by using arm-locks, elbow-joint locks or strangle and choke techniques to gain a submission.

The maximum score for a holding technique is won thirty seconds after it is considered to be effective and well and truly secured. The successful application of a hold is indicated when the referee calls *osaekomi*. This is an indication to the timekeeper to start the count-down and informs the spectators and also the competitors that a standard immobilizing hold-down has been put into effect. If the person being held manages to break out within the thirty-seconds span, then the referee calls *toketa* and a score below *ippon* will be given depending on the time the hold was effective. If such a break-out occurs the contest continues and further holds, arm-locks or strangles can be attempted.

A player's aim should always be to try to dominate his opponent and remain over him, without being dominated himself. In attack the body should be used to the best advantage in order to control or pin down an opponent. Anticipate the moves an opponent will make to try to break free. In defence endeavour to avoid being held or caught by the ultimate technique and constantly try to get out of trouble and turn the tables by switching as quickly as possible from defence to attack.

A vast range of moves is linked to or surrounds the standard holds, arm-locks and strangles, and there is no end to the tactics and tricks that can be learned. Unlike *tachiwaza, newaza* (groundwork techniques) can give the judo enthusiast years of competitive activity. Craft learned in groundwork can stand him in good stead long after his best competition days are over. Indeed, many of the older or veteran *judoka* are renowned for their groundwork skill, and many an old warrior has built up a reputation for his skill in *newaza.*

In *tachiwaza* a player usually develops just two or three match-winning throws, but in groundwork a good *newaza* specialist usually has a greater range of moves and techniques. You can never learn too much groundwork.

The mark of a good groundwork specialist is that he conserves energy by making or encouraging his opponent to do all the work. In shifting from one position to another, he does not leave weak gaps through which his opponent can find an opening and get out of trouble. Complete beginners tend to strain every muscle and stiffen every limb as they hold an opponent. This drains the energy reserves, and because the player is completely stiff he can easily be turned when his opponent tries to turn or roll him off. Only constant groundwork practice will overcome this.

Beginners also tend to try to control their opponent's hands and arms when it is really his trunk that should first be contained. In attempting an *osaekomiwaza* (holding technique), hold your opponent firmly on his back; trapping or 'tying up' his limbs will follow naturally.

Arm-locks and strangles show *newaza* is far more advanced than pure wrestling and grappling. Though judo has only a small number of these techniques, the possible variations are limitless. Such techniques are decisive and applied unexpectedly provide an exciting 'sudden-death' dimension; of course they usually result in the ultimate score, since an opponent can only submit – unless he wants a severely damaged arm or to be strangled completely.

Holding and grappling techniques are perfectly safe for children to practise under supervision – as with all aspects of judo. They should not be allowed to practise arm-locks and strangles until they understand what they are doing and that uncontrolled enthusiasm and excitement can cause serious accidents.

Practice each technique a number of times and on opponents of different size. The variations on each hold depend on the size of an opponent. As soon as you have a fair idea of the hold and have practised it to both left and right, move onto the best methods of escaping from the hold. This will not only enliven groundwork practice but will also expose the advantages and weaknesses of each hold.

Kesagatame (scarf hold)

Kesagatame is the best hold for the beginner to tackle first. Not only is it easy to understand but it is used at all levels.

The weakest point is invariably when *uke* tries to bridge and twist over in the direction of his own left shoulder. *Tori* should be constantly alive to this threat and have his right hand ready to release its grip and create a prop by extending the arm straight and placing the palm of the right hand on the mat at a point some eighteen inches from *uke's* left ear. This will frustrate any bridging action, but once *uke's* efforts to bridge in that direction have been exhausted *tori* should return his right hand to its original grip. *Tori* must sense when *uke* is going to bridge and in which direction he will attempt to escape. Only constant practice will achieve such awareness. In using this prop against the bridge, *tori* must also be sure that his right fore-arm will not be trapped at the back of *uke's* neck: an experienced opponent could bridge and at the same time use his head and the back of his neck to keep his opponent's right arm trapped.

A variation of this hold is *makurakesagatame,* in which *tori,* instead of gripping *uke's* right sleeve at the bicep, grips his own right inner thigh, thus raising *uke's* head off the mat and frustrating any bridging attempt.

Kesagatame

Sitting alongside *uke* and making sure that there is no gap between his own hips and *uke's* trunk, *tori* should spread his legs to give a firm wide base. With the outside of his right leg pressing into the mat, his left leg bent with knee up and his left foot placed well back, *tori* should be ready to move round the mat as *uke* struggles. He must never allow a gap to appear between his right hip and *uke's* trunk.

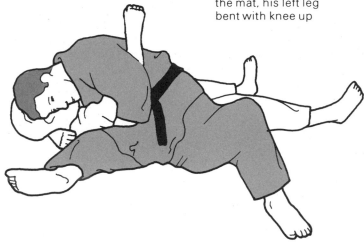

Tori grips with his right arm as far around *uke's* neck as possible, holding *uke's* jacket with his right hand at *uke's* right shoulder. *Tori* should at the same time secure *uke's* right arm by clasping *uke's* wrist high under his armpit, using his left hand to grasp *uke's* sleeve just above the elbow. *Tori's* hands should now grip as if they were pulling against each other. If *tori* is smaller than *uke* he should keep his head and shoulders well down towards the mat; if he is bigger he can afford to use his weight by lying more across *uke's* chest.

Dave Starbrook, 5th Dan
Olympic silver medallist 1972, Olympic bronze medallist 1976, nine times British Open Champion, British Olympic Team Manager.

Kesagatame

'I chose *taiotoshi* because I was not supple enough to do most of the other techniques. *Taiotoshi* suited me ideally and I had the power to do my particular straight-legged style. *Kesagatame* came as a natural and fitting progression and follow-up from *taiotoshi* if the throw did not score the maximum *ippon.*'

A further variation is *kuzurekesagatame* (broken scarf hold). *Tori* passes his right arm through *uke's* left armpit and with his right hand cupped palm upwards grips *uke's* left shoulder. *Tori's* right hand is then ready to twist palm downwards and press flat on the mat if *uke* struggles and attempts to bridge. This action eliminates the weakness of pure *kesagatame* but in so doing opens up possibilities in other areas. In general *kuzure* is favoured by the bigger and heavier *judoka.* As in all scarf techniques, the smaller man, besides thinking about all the possibilities of escape, must keep his head and shoulders as near to the mat as possible, with his head turned to his left and almost touching his own right knee.

Kuzurekesa-gatame

Sitting alongside *uke* and making sure that there is no gap between his own right hip and *uke's* trunk, *tori* should spread his legs in order to give a firm, strong base. His left leg should lie flat and the outside of his right leg should press into the mat. *Tori* should then pass his right arm through *uke's* left armpit and under

uke's left shoulder, palm upwards, so that it grips *uke's* shoulder. With his right hand cupped over *uke's* left shoulder, *tori* should then secure *uke's* right arm by gripping his wrist high under his own left armpit, reinforcing by holding *uke's* sleeve just above the right elbow with his left hand. *Tori* pulls himself in close across *uke's* chest with his right hand cupped over *uke's* left shoulder. He should be prepared to use his right hand as a prop when *uke* attempts to bridge *tori* over his own left shoulder.

Ushirokesagatame *(reverse scarf hold)*

Some people call this the rear scarf hold, but 'reverse' describes it better. It is distinctly different in that *tori* sits facing *uke's* feet. This hold is not as common as the others in the *kesa* family but is favoured by bigger and heavier *judoka.*

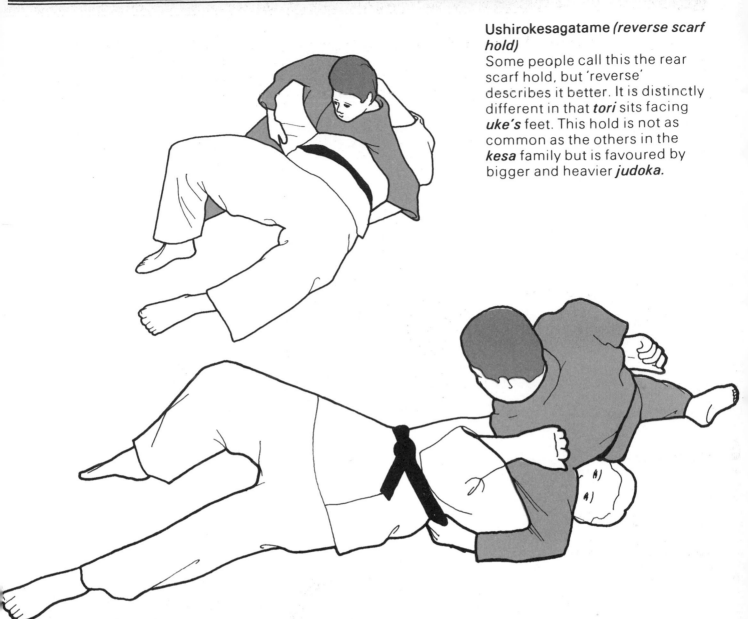

Ushiro-kesagatame

Tori's action in this hold are like those in *kesagatame*, but in this case *tori* sits reversed, facing *uke's* feet. Sitting alongside *uke's* head with legs well spread and firmly placed, *tori* passes his left hand under *uke's* shoulder and grips *uke's* belt at the left side of *uke's* waist. *Tori's* right arm clasps *uke's* right forearm under *uke's* armpit, keeping *uke's* right arm bent and supporting the armpit grip by gripping *uke's* right sleeve just above the elbow. *Tori* should lie back, slightly trapping *uke's* head but keeping his own chin in to his own chest, to strengthen the hold. He should make sure that his weight bears down on *uke's* chest.

Kamishihogatame

There are two styles for this hold, used according to the opponent's size. If your opponent is bigger than you, take up a crouched position, if he is smaller, then lie flat and use all your weight.

Lying face down with the top of his head towards *uke's* feet and with chests touching, *tori* should take both his arms under *uke's* shoulders and grip the belt with both hands at the sides of the waist. *Tori* should not lie too high on *uke's* chest and should hold with both elbows pinched in under *uke's* shoulders. As *uke* struggles to escape, *tori* should keep his own body in line with *uke's* and lie with the side of his head pinned to *uke's* upper chest.

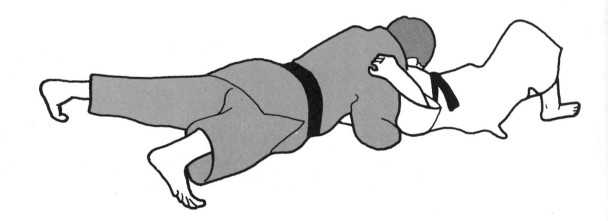

Kamishihogatame *(upper four quarters hold)*

There are two distinct styles, used according to *tori's* size in relation to his opponent. In both, the hands pass under *uke's* shoulders and grip *uke's* belt at the side of *uke's* waist. If *tori* gripped underneath, *uke* could cause considerable pain to *tori's* knuckles as he tried to escape. In heavyweight judo, *uke's* head should be trapped between *tori's* left elbow and trunk. *Tori* should lie flat with legs spread apart. In lightweight judo, *tori* should kneel up on his right knee and extend his left leg out as a prop. He should be ready to switch the propping action quckly from one leg to the other depending on *uke's* attempts to escape. As in all holds where *tori* is face down, his hips should be kept parallel to the ground and his toes curled under. This is very important, both to avoid a succession of mat burns on the instep of the foot and also to provide greater mobility with the legs.

Kuzurekamishi-hogatame

The term broken upper four quarters does not mean that the hold is broken or in any way weak. Indeed, some may find this hold even stronger than *kamishihogatame*. The hold can be effected either in the crouch position or lying flat face down, according to the opponent's size. The left-hand grip is the same as in *kamishihogatame*, *tori's* left arm passing under *uke's* left shoulder and his left hand gripping *uke's* belt at the side of the waist. *Tori's* right arm passes over *uke's* right shoulder, down through *uke's* right armpit and back under to *uke's* collar behind the neck. Holding with his right hand, with fingers inside *uke's* collar, *tori* should keep his body in line with *uke's* as *uke* struggles to break the hold.

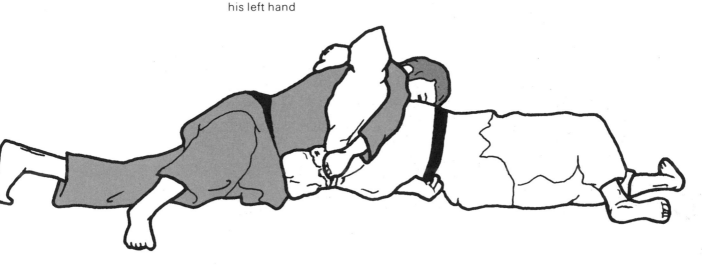

A further variation of this hold, perhaps more popular, is *kuzurekamishihogatame* (broken upper four quarters hold). In this case *tori* holds conventionally with his left hand but passes his right hand through *uke's* right armpit, taking it up to *uke's* collar behind his neck and gripping inside the collar with his fingers.

In both these holds *tori* should endeavour to keep his body in line with *uke's*, for if *uke* is able to twist his body at right angles he will bridge and escape or even get his arms between his own and his opponent's body and work himself free.

93

Katagatame *(shoulder hold)*
This hold is best effected when *uke* gets his right arm free while being held in *kesagatame.* To escape from *kesagatame* he pushes under *tori's* chin in an attempt to force *tori's* head back whereupon *tori* moves into *katagatame.* Correctly applied a strangle also results from this hold – many a contest has been won in this way.

Katagatame
Kneeling alongside *uke* with his right knee placed firmly against *uke's* side, *tori's* right arm holds *uke* round his neck, at the same time pushing *uke's* right upper arm against *uke's* face.

Tori then places the right side of his head against the back of his own left hand. He slides the left hand out, his head keeping the pressure on *uke's* right arm, and grips his own right hand behind *uke's* neck.

Tori uses his left leg as a prop to reinforce the hold. *Tori* should keep his own head well down towards the mat; in fact his forehead should touch the mat throughout the hold.

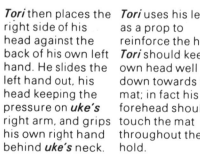

Yokoshihogatame *(side four quarters hold)*

Though this hold does not at first seem as strong as others, with training and experience it can become a very powerful technique.

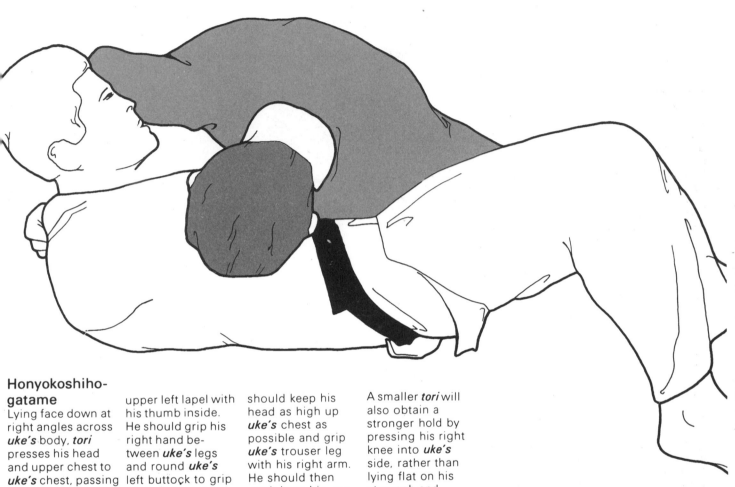

Honyokoshiho-gatame

Lying face down at right angles across *uke's* body, *tori* presses his head and upper chest to *uke's* chest, passing his left hand under and behind *uke's* neck to grip *uke's* upper left lapel with his thumb inside. He should grip his right hand be-tween *uke's* legs and round *uke's* left buttock to grip *uke's* belt at the side. If *tori* is smaller than *uke* he should keep his head as high up *uke's* chest as possible and grip *uke's* trouser leg with his right arm. He should then straighten his arm, so pinning *uke's* trousers to the mat. A smaller *tori* will also obtain a stronger hold by pressing his right knee into *uke's* side, rather than lying flat on his stomach and stretching out his legs.

Tateshihogatame *(vertical four quarters hold)*
This hold is very different from the rest and needs a lot of practice. In a stronger variation, *tori* can trap *uke's* left arm by pressing it between the side or back of his head and *uke's* own head.

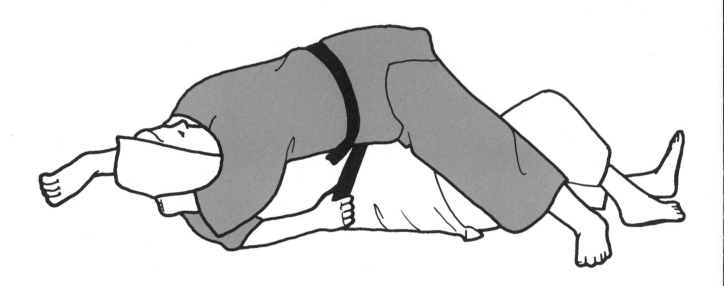

Tateshihoga-tame

In this hold, *tori* straddles *uke*, who is lying on his back. Ducking his head under *uke's* further arm (in this case his left), *tori* drives up with his head, forcing *uke's* left arm up alongside *uke's* head. Locking his knees in to grip *uke's* trunk, *tori* then locks his feet under *uke's* upper thighs.

Hugging *uke's* neck with his left arm, *tori* grips *uke's* collar as far round as he can with his left hand, keeping *uke's* left arm locked against *uke's* head with the back of his own head. A number of different right hand grips are open to *tori* and they should all be tried.

He can grip his own left sleeve behind *uke's* head, he can take his right hand down to *uke's* belt and grip it at the side and slightly to the back, he can transfer his left-hand grip from behind *uke's* collar to his own right lapel, leaving his right arm free to act as a prop as *uke* tries to bridge.

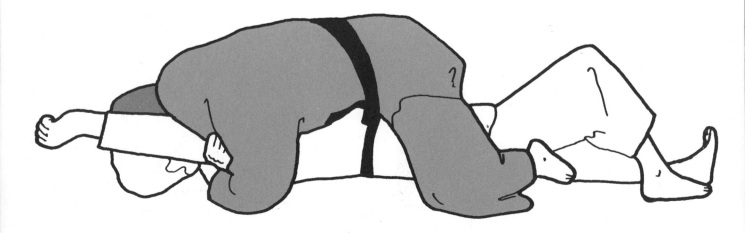

CHAPTER 17. KANSETSUWAZA – ARM-LOCK TECHNIQUES

Arm-locks and strangles can be attempted in *tachiwaza* but are not often successful because, since the opponent is on his feet, he can, if he is quick enough, twist or turn away from the attempt. Nevertheless, these techniques should be practised as much as possible in standing judo, for they are the essence of surprise and are less demanding physically. This is very important in international judo: in an average tournament at national or international level, a competitor might go through between seven and ten contests before reaching the finals. A few physically easy wins on the way will leave him fresh for the most important contest.

Udegarami *(arm entanglement)*
In *udegarami tori* seizes *uke's* right wrist with his right hand, pinning the back of *uke's* right forearm to the mat. Passing his left forearm under *uke's* upper arm, *tori* should grip his own right wrist and then with both hands slowly force *uke's* elbow over towards *uke's* head (see version A).

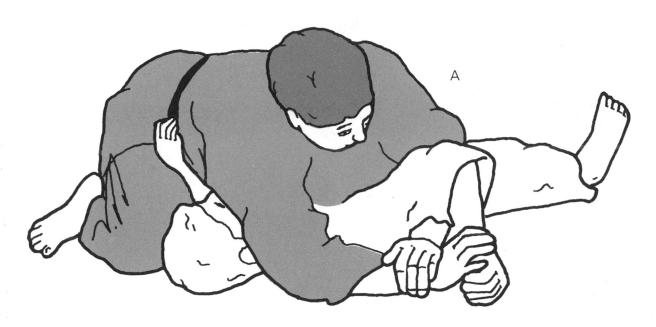

A

Udegarami

Arm entanglement is a good technique to use when *uke* tries to ward off *tori* in the struggle for supremacy on the ground. Shown in version A, in trying to pin *uke* on his back, *tori* seizes the wrist of *uke's* further arm. With one hand he grips *uke's* right wrist and, passing his free hand under *uke's* right upper arm, takes hold of his own wrist keeping his palm down against the outside of *uke's* wrist.

Keeping *uke's* left arm bent, *tori* slowly but firmly pushes *uke's* arm down to the mat. He then pulls slowly down with both hands towards *uke's* feet until *uke* submits, remaining face down across *uke's* chest throughout. Version B is an alternative.

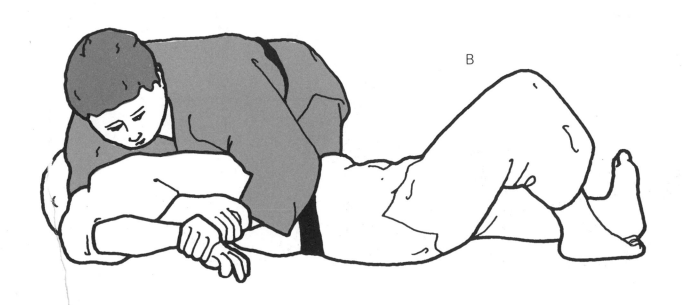

B

Udegatame *(cross arm-lock)*

This is possible in standing judo but must be executed very quickly in order to achieve surprise. There are many opportunities for **udegatame** in **newaza,** but (as with all arm-locks) it is important to ease the arm-lock on slowly and not jerk or snap the arm back suddenly in the early stages of training.

Udegatame

This arm-lock can be attempted from a number of positions. The most common is when *tori* is crouched or kneeling over his opponent who is on his back. As *uke*

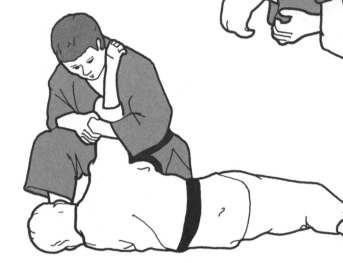

attempts to fend off with his further arm and tries to turn on to his left side, *tori* seizes *uke's* outstretched right arm by placing the palm of his left hand on *uke's* elbow and then the palm of his

right hand on the back of his own left hand.
He slides *uke's* wrist against the left side of his own head and hunches his left shoulder so that *uke's* wrist is locked against his neck.

Tori then rolls *uke's* elbow to make sure that the arm is kept straight. Finally he pulls *uke's* arm into his own chest with both hands to effect the arm-lock.

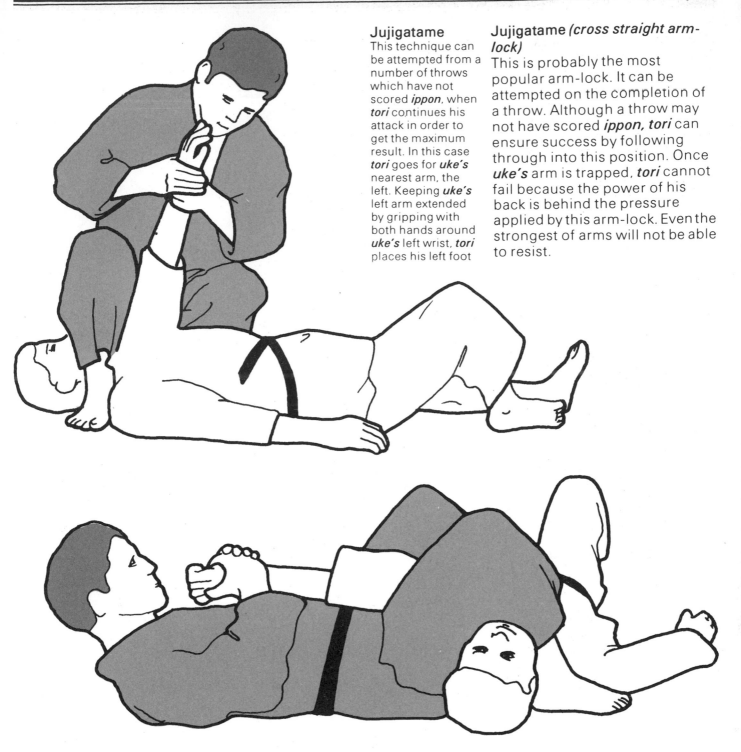

Jujigatame
This technique can be attempted from a number of throws which have not scored *ippon*, when *tori* continues his attack in order to get the maximum result. In this case *tori* goes for *uke's* nearest arm, the left. Keeping *uke's* left arm extended by gripping with both hands around *uke's* left wrist, *tori* places his left foot

Jujigatame *(cross straight arm-lock)*
This is probably the most popular arm-lock. It can be attempted on the completion of a throw. Although a throw may not have scored *ippon*, *tori* can ensure success by following through into this position. Once *uke's* arm is trapped, *tori* cannot fail because the power of his back is behind the pressure applied by this arm-lock. Even the strongest of arms will not be able to resist.

Ellen Cobb, 4th Dan
Women's British Open Champion several times, European silver (twice) and bronze medallist, British international many times.

Jujigatame
'I think this is a very useful technique, it certainly has been for me. It can be used at the end of almost any throwing technique, regardless of the score, less than *ippon*. Even if the throw is successful there is the possibility of a dispute but if you continue through into *jujigatame* it guarantees success. I like this technique because it is a fluent movement and a natural follow-up from *tachiwaza*.'

firmly against *uke's* side. He then steps over *uke's* head, placing his right heel against *uke's* neck.
Tori then sits down as close as possible to *uke*, sliding *uke's* outstretched arm up between his own legs.
As *tori* lies back to effect the arm-lock he should make sure that the thumb of *uke's* left hand is

placed upwards. Laying *uke's* left arm along his groin, *tori* grips the hand of *uke's* outstretched arm and, pulling it slowly to his own chest, raises his hips off the mat. The power of *tori's* back will ensure that the arm-lock brings about a quick submission.

99

CHAPTER 18. SHIMEWAZA – STRANGLE TECHNIQUES

Hadakajime *(naked strangle)*

This strangle is very simple to apply. It is attempted from behind the opponent.

The signal for submission should always be given clearly and distinctly, and *tori* should then release the pressure immediately. As with arm-locks, strangles should never be practised or attempted without a qualified instructor being present so that if *uke* does pass out the correct resuscitation procedure can be carried out immediately.

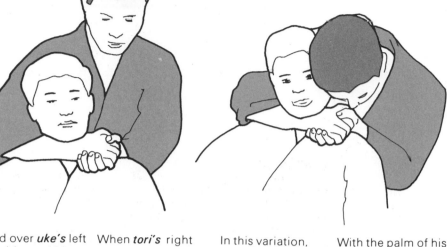

Hadakajime

This technique is called naked strangle because there is no need to use the opponent's jacket. It comes from behind and as in all such

techniques *tori* must first make sure that he controls *uke's* body by locking his legs around his waist. With palm upwards *tori* passes his left

hand over *uke's* left shoulder and his right over *uke's* right shoulder, boring his way between *uke's* chin and neck with the knuckles of his right hand.

When *tori's* right hand meets with his own left hand, *tori* stiffens his right hand, putting it in the palm of his left hand and pulling with both arms towards his own chest.

In this variation, instead of gripping his own left hand *tori* grips his lower left bicep and passes his left hand up to the back of *uke's* neck.

With the palm of his left hand against the back of *uke's* head, *tori* pushes *uke's* head forward to make sure that the strangle is effective.

Katajujijime *(single cross strangle)*

Although it is more common in *newaza,* this strangle has been known to succeed in *tachiwaza.*

Katajujijime

This strangle is attempted from the front, with *uke* and *tori* face to face. When prone *tori*

should straddle *uke* and clamp his

knees tight around *uke's* trunk, tucking his toes in and gripping behind the

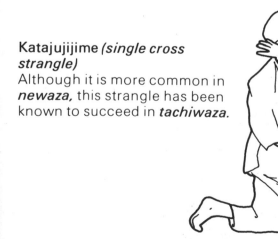
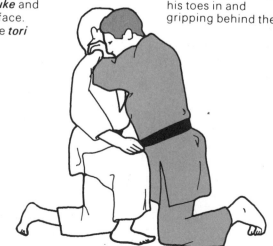

Gyakujujijime *(reverse cross strangle)*

This strangle is similar to *katajujijime* except that the fingers of both hands are placed inside the lapel. In groundwork, always try to control an opponent's body by trapping him between the legs, so that he cannot twist or turn out of the technique.

Gyakujujijime

This reverse cross strangle is attempted from the front and can equally well be carried out when both contestants are on their feet, provided *tori* is clever enough to slide both hands in deep before *uke* can react. In practising this technique with *uke* in a prone position, *tori* should straddle *uke* and crossing his hands palms upwards should slide them deep to each side of *uke's* collar, gripping the jacket with fingers inside and thumbs outside.

Then, lying forward close to *uke* with his head buried deep alongside *uke's* head, *tori* then puts the pressure on the carotid arteries on each side of *uke's* neck by pulling down with his hands and out with his elbows. *Uke* may attempt to roll, but *tori* should persevere, keeping his legs locked round *uke's* body until *uke* submits.

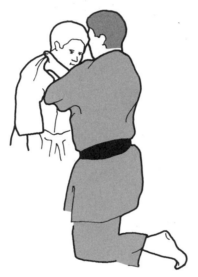

upper part of *uke's* thighs. *Tori* slides his left hand up, palm upwards, the back of his hand brushing *uke's* chest, to grip, with fingers inside, *uke's* left lapel.

Gripping as high round the collar as possible, *tori* then crosses his right hand over the forearm of his left and with thumb inside *uke's* right collar grips *uke's* right lapel, again as high as possible.

Lying well forward, *tori* then puts on pressure by pulling down with his hands and out with his elbows.

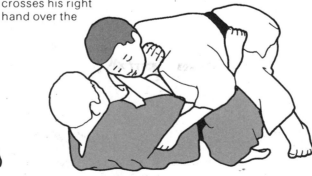

Namijujijime

This is a strangle from the front similar to *gyakujujijime* and *katajujijime*. Passing his left hand across *uke's* chest he slides his thumb inside *uke's* left lapel and high towards the neck. Crossing his right hand over the front of *uke*, *tori* then grips *uke's* right lapel with his right hand, thumb inside. With *uke* in a prone position *tori* should straddle *uke* locking his legs tight around *uke's* trunk, and then exert pressure on *uke's* neck by lying forward on his own forearms and driving his elbows up over *uke's* shoulders and pressing them into the mat. Some people find this strangle works better if they pull down with their hands and elbows

out to the side. Experiment to find the best method and the one that works quickest depending on the type of opponent. If an opponent attempts to move between *tori's* legs in order to hold *tori* down on his back, it is an ideal opportunity to try this strangle from underneath.

Okurierijime *(sliding lapel strangle)*

In this strangle, pressure is put on not by pulling with the elbows outwards but by straightening the arms. The strangle is then almost instant.

These strangles have a number of variations, but these are the most commonly used and the most practical under contest conditions.

Okurierijime

This is a strangle from behind and in contests should always be attempted with *tori's* legs locked around *uke* from behind to prevent *uke* escaping during the preparation for the strangle. *Tori's* left hand must pass between *uke's* left arm and trunk and should grip and pull down *uke's* left lapel. *Tori's* right hand passes over *uke's* right shoulder and grips high, with thumb inside, at *uke's* left lapel. *Tori's* left hand should ensure that he can get his right-hand grip deep around *uke's* neck.

Tori then passes his left hand across *uke's* chest to grip high at *uke's* right lapel, again with thumb inside. To achieve pressure for the strangle, *tori* should straighten his arms without pulling out to the sides.

Katahajime

In the preparation stage this single-wing neck lock is similar to the sliding lapel neck-lock. As it is a strangle from behind *tori* should always first lock his legs round *uke* from behind. He passes his left hand between *uke's* left arm and trunk and grips *uke's* left lapel, pulling the lapel downwards and tight, so that his right hand, passing over *uke's* right shoulder, can slide up high round the left side of *uke's* neck, the right thumb inside the collar so as to establish a strong, tight grip high on the lapel or collar. *Tori's* left hand now thrusts forward and upwards in a big push which drives *uke's* left arm up in the air, it comes to rest on the back of *uke's* neck. *Tori* then completes the strangle by exerting pressure on *uke's* left carotid artery with his right hand and pushing *uke's* head forward on to the strangle with his left hand.

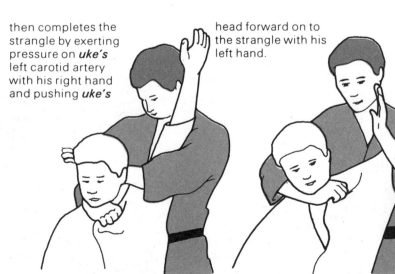

Judo has outstripped its ju-jutsu origins and emerged as an Olympic sport because it can be played in freestyle competition according to rules that render it combative but safe. Kodokan judo has always attached priority to safe practice, but the modern rules for the conduct of competition only crystallized with the formation of the International Judo Federation. Previously the standard of *shiai* (tournament) outside Japan was poor; there were few contestants and they were inexperienced because of the general lack of competitive outlets. The basic Kodokan rules were interpreted in the Japanese spirit as it was understood by high-grade players who had trained there, but for many years there was no official judo rule book in English. Translations were made for personal use, but they were not widely circularized.

All that has now changed and the modern IJF rules govern contest judo throughout the world. The IJF requirements as to the *shiaijo* (contest area) and its personnel are observed at all major tournaments. At a prestige event there may be five or more such areas in use simultaneously in order to cope effectively with the preliminary rounds. Every competition area should be a minimum of 14m square and a maximum of 16m

Aerial view of an official contest area conforming to International Judo Federation rules as to dimensions and officials.

square. Within this overall dimension are a contest mat with a distinctively coloured (usually bright red) internal margin and an external safety zone not forming part of the combat area, although *tori* (the thrower) can score from an attack which spills over into this zone provided he himself has not stepped out. The inner contest area should be either 9m or 10m square with a safety surround of never less than 2.5m, except where adjacent mats share a common safety area on one side, when a single-width safety strip is acceptable. There are heavy penalties for players who carry on a contest outside the combat area and the presence of a 1m wide internal margin is intended to give ample warning of the risk of leaving the area.

The officials who administer a contest comprise a referee, two judges, a timekeeper and a recorder. The referee stays in the area with the contestants and has sole responsibility for the conduct of a contest and the announcement of a result. His pronouncements are final so far as the players are concerned, and etiquette demands that they accept his rulings with the utmost good grace whatever their own standing in the sport. In reaching his decisions the referee is subject to immediate review by the two judges. Each judge can signal his disagreement with any decision, and if both of them contradict the referee but are agreed between themselves they can substitute their dissenting opinion for his. A judge can always signal to the referee should something have been overlooked during the contest, but in every case the referee's decision prevails unless the two judges are agreed to the contrary.

The judges face one another at opposite corners of the mat;

The Longines electronic scoreboard in use. With 1 min 46 secs of a contest left the 30 illuminated bulbs at the top of the board indicate that a player has just scored *ippon* by holding his opponent down for 30 seconds. Every lighted bulb signifies the passing of 1 second. After 9 seconds the bulbs registering further time are of a different colour showing that whatever happens thereafter *koka* has been scored. Similar colour changes occur to indicate *yuko* and *waza-ari* respectively. All earlier scores are presented as running totals in the appropriate panels on the board. The player wearing red is marked on the right-hand side of the board, the other (wearing white) appears on the left. In this case red had scored a single *koka*, while white had a *yuko* and a *koka* to his credit. No penalties were recorded in this contest. Had there been any, the relevant oblong panel would have been illuminated alongside the name of the penalty awarded. During the contest penalties are shown against the penalized player's score, at the end they are transferred over as a positive score to the opponent.

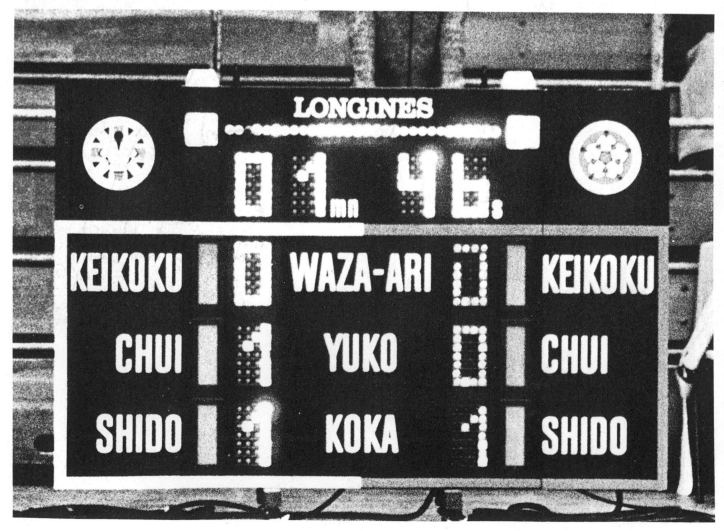

their function is to assist the referee to reach a correct decision on the facts as they unfold and on matters of interpretation of the rules. From their corner seats the judges have an unobstructed view down two different sides of the mat. If a contest carries over into the safety area the appropriate judge must advise the referee so that he can

A Russian Man-of-war: Shota Chochoshvilli waits for an opponent to take the mat. Notice the additional white belt for identification purposes. The modern judo player wears his *judogi* long in the sleeves and leg.

disregard the surplus activity for scoring purposes and penalize a contestant if necessary. When scores are even at the end of a match, the referee calls on the judges to deliver *hantei* (judgement). Each then indicates by means of a flag the competitor whom he thinks displayed *yuseigachi* (superiority). In the event of disagreement, the referee has the casting vote.

Judo competitions take the form of a series of matches each fought to a decision during the time allotted. The time fixed by the organizers in advance may not be less than three minutes nor more than twenty minutes. At an average promotion examination the lower grades will compete in three-minute contests and higher grades will fight for four minutes; preliminary rounds in the British Open Championships last six minutes with ten-minute contests in the finals; fifteen minutes is the time appropriate for the level of an Olympic final. In certain circumstances the pre-arranged contest time can be extended if it proves impossible to reach a fair decision on the available evidence. The times quoted refer to the period during which the contestants are actually fighting for a score; injury time or time spent re-arranging the *judogi* is deducted on the referee's instruction (*jikan* – time-out). The timekeeper stops the clock voluntarily whenever the referee temporarily suspends the bout by calling *matte* (wait), if, for instance, he wishes to bring the players back to the centre of the mat. It is also the timekeeper's duty to keep account of the time spent escaping from any *osaekomiwaza*, because partial scores can be earned with short hold downs.

The contest recorder causes a visual record to be displayed of the scoring position for and against each contestant at every stage of the contest; everyone, including the players, is able to ascertain who is showing superiority during and at the end of the match. A custom-built electronic scoreboard is used for this purpose at national and international events. At least one display panel is sited beside each mat area enabling scores, penalties, time of hold-downs and time unexpired to be digested at a glance. The same result is achieved by the use of less sophisticated manual equipment at minor championships.

When two contestants are called to the mat, the first-named puts a thin red tape around his waist in addition to his own coloured belt for purposes of identification; his opponent wears a similar white tape. Both then approach the area according to their identifying colour: red from the left as seen from the control table, white from the right. When the judges are in position the referee will invite the players to take up a standing position facing one another approximately 4m apart at the centre of the mat. At this juncture experienced players show respect by bowing crisply to the referee. Without waiting to be told, each then bows to the other and on the command *hajime* (begin) the contest gets under way.

Japanese words of command and interim scores and penalties are called aloud as the contest progresses: *matte* (wait); *sonomama* (freeze in that position); *yoshi* (carry on fighting); *jikan* (stop the clock); *sore made* (that is all, finish). Each has a corresponding arm signal so that the recorder and timekeeper can follow what is happening above the noise of the crowd. Regardless of any announcement from the timekeeper, the contest is not at an end until the referee calls *sore made*. Neither contestant may leave the area without the referee's permission and it is prohibited under the rules to disregard a legitimate instruction. A contestant is liable to disqualification or other disciplinary action on breaching the rules. Arguing with the referee can in due course attract a period of suspension from contest judo.

The contentious part of a referee's work is the allocation of scores and penalties. A score of *ippon* (full point) has already been described as symbolic death, and in keeping with the analogy it brings a contest to an immediate end. *Ippon* is given to the contestant who deliberately and with impetus throws his opponent flat on his back or who skilfully lifts him from a prone position on the mat to shoulder height. In groundwork the same score is achieved by immobilizing an opponent for thirty seconds by use of *osaekomiwaza*. Its effectiveness may be obvious because of a submission (signalled by calling out or by tapping opponent or mat with hand or foot at least twice in quick succession) or because of its consequences.

Waza-ari (almost *ippon*) is given for a throw that does not quite warrant the full score or a hold that has lasted twenty-five but less than thirty seconds. It is a cumulative score in as much as a second *waza-ari* to a single contestant finishes the contest by *waza-ari awasete ippon* (*ippon* by stages). *Yuko* (almost *waza-ari*) and *koka* (almost *yuko*) are awarded for both throws and groundwork techniques. The right award in the case of a throw is a matter of judgement but in groundwork it is more clear cut: *yuko* for a hold lasting twenty but less than twenty-five seconds; *koka* for one lasting ten but less than twenty seconds. Unlike *waza-ari,* these scores are not cumulative. One *yuko* outpoints twenty *koka;* one *waza-ari* is superior to twenty *yuko*.

In relation to throws, but not groundwork, the referee must exercise his discretion in assessing the correct score. If care were not taken one referee's *yuko* could easily become another's *waza-ari;* to counteract this referees and judges have erred on the side of caution with the result that it has become significantly more difficult to achieve *ippon* and to a lesser extent *waza-ari* with a throw than was the case when they were the only two scores in use.

Ouchigari is a subordinate element in many combination sequences. As is shown here, it rarely produces a major score in its own right under contest conditions.

Simultaneously a range of penalties has been introduced, each of which translates into a positive score for the non-penalized contestant at the end of the contest. Less discretion is exercisable over these penalties. Consequently a player can sometimes break the rules out of carelessness and give his opponent the equivalent of *waza-ari* on a plate, when that opponent might have had great difficulty in winning that score outright.

The penalties that can be awarded and their values as a positive score are as follows:

Shido, worth *koka* to the opponent, is imposed for a minor breach of the rules.

A further minor breach or a moderate breach of the rules attracts a penalty of *chui,* worth *yuko* to the opponent.

A further moderate breach or a serious breach of the rules attracts a penalty of *keikoku,* worth *waza-ari* to the opponent.

A further serious breach or a grave breach of the rules attracts a penalty of *hansoku make* or disqualification, worth *ippon* to the opponent.

To an opponent who has, or subsequently obtains, a score of *waza-ari, keikoku* is worth *ippon sogo gachi* (compound win by *ippon*).Successive penalties erase all lesser penalties, which are removed from the scoreboard and left out of account when a result must be declared on the basis of superiority. For the purpose of imposing a penalty the referee will stop the contest and will inform the judges of his intention. In the case of *keikoku* or *hansoku make* the offender is made to kneel while the referee publicly dishonours him.

Apart from a deliberate foul, the deadliest sin in contest judo is to leave the area without the referee's permission. Hence the conspicuous danger zone to warn contestants of their whereabouts on the mat. The rules provide for a penalty to be awarded against a contestant who:
(i)   deliberately leaves the contest area;
(ii) pretends to apply a technique in order to leave the area;
(iii) intentionally and contrary to the spirit of judo throws his opponent out;

(iv) forces his opponent to leave the area;

(v) leaves the area because of his own efforts to upset his opponent's balance.

In every case except (v) the penalty is *keikoku*; in case (v) it is *chui*. The only occasion on which a player is not penalized is when he leaves the area through no fault whatsoever of his own.

Experienced players know that when a contest is being fought on the red margin they are running the risk of a penalty. For all that, it is not 'contrary to the spirit of judo' to attack with *nage waza* and *katame waza* inside the area; a technique that is successful will score even though the opponent happens to leave the area in the process; the exit is incidental to the throw and not an objective in its own right. Nevertheless the distinction is a fine one, especially when the technique in question was not decisive. The referee must ask himself whether the exit was incidental to the judo or blameworthy, and if blameworthy, who is to blame. The gamble is that the opponent might be penalized to an attractive value if the referee feels he was to blame for taking the contest out of the area; experienced line players could win an award for making it look as though they are innocent and the other side guilty, but novices should not be tempted to follow suit. There is too much at stake for amateur line fighting.

A warning must also be given against the adoption of an excessively defensive attitude in contest, because this too is prohibited by the rules. A 'state of non-combativity may be taken to exist when in general for 20 or 30 seconds there have been no attacking moves on the part of one or either or both contestants' (IJF commentary to rule 30). At first the referee will warn a player without penalizing him. He does so by rotating his hands around one another at chest height so that the judges and officials know there has been a warning. Thereafter the usual ascending scale of penalties applies. The comment quoted refers to genuine and not merely token attacks and the relevant time limits can be adjusted according to circumstance. The moral of all this is clear: know the rules and fight hard and fast within them.

CHAPTER 20.   ASSESSMENTS AND COMPETITIVE GRADINGS

The first species of contest encountered by a newcomer to judo is bound to be a promotion examination. It will in all probability be held either at the student's own club in his early days or at a larger club in the same district; the opposition is likely to be drawn from the membership of clubs in the immediate locality, and the qualified examiner and referee in charge of the proceedings will be high grades who teach or have some other connection with the area concerned.

Details have already been given (in Chapter 5) of the grades for which the players will be competing. The idea of ranking players by grade is peculiar to judo the Olympic sport but commonplace in judo as a Japanese recreation. It is possible to hold a *dan* grade in Japan in activities as diverse as flower arranging, archery and intellectual board games.

Kyu grade examinations involve very little red tape. The candidate need only possess a current BJA licence and have allowed at least fifty-six days to elapse since his last examination in order to turn up and participate. The exact procedure adopted varies from place to place, but the usual practice is to classify participants by grade and sex as they book in so as to produce groups of compatible names from which the contestants can be drawn. Candidates pay a small fee for entering, change into their *judogi* and then wait near the mat area for further instructions. In the lull before the examinations get under way the examinees may use the mat to perform loosening-up exercises. While waiting their turn they should keep warm by wearing a track-suit, or something similar, and a thick pair of socks.

The selection of contestants is quite arbitrary and it is not unusual for a lightweight to find himself up against a heavyweight. Where possible, examiners do try to prevent gross disparities occurring and to avoid matching players from the same club, because undeserved stalemate can result when two players are familiar with each other's style. Every candidate is given two or three contests against opponents of the same grade in which to prove his ability. At grades below 1st *Kyu* the examinee must win at least one contest before he can be considered for promotion; the only scores recorded for this purpose are *ippon* and *waza-ari*. It must be stressed that one win is the bare minimum; promotion will not inevitably follow, but by the same token it is possible for a candidate to advance two grades if his performance is outstanding. The examiner can put such a person in with the candidates for the next higher grade if he thinks it desirable. At *kyu* grade examinations the players who are successful in the practical part of the assessment go on to take the theory part on the same day. It is still possible to fail with a dismal performance in this section.

The process of obtaining promotion for candidates of 1st *Kyu* and above is stricter and more complex. Various time limits within the grades and minimum age requirements must be complied with and there are alternative methods of earning promotion to and within the *dan* degree: the candidate may accumulate points in point-scoring events up to the figure

THE INTER-RELATIONSHIP OF FACTORS RELEVANT TO PROMOTION BY ACCUMULATION OF POINTS, TO AND WITHIN THE DAN DEGREE

From:		1st *kyu*	1st *dan*	2nd *dan*	3rd *dan*	4th *dan*
To:		1st *dan*	2nd *dan*	3rd *dan*	4th *dan*	5th *dan*
Minimum age:		15 years	17 years	19 years	22 years	26 years
Points prescribed:		Minimum time to be spent at present grade:				
Candidates under 30 years	200	---	1 year	18 months	2 years	3 years
	150	---	2 years	3 years	4 years	5 years
	100	6 months*	3 years	4 years	6 years	7 years
Candidates over 30 years	100	6 months	1 year	2 years	3 years	4 years
	75	18 months	2 years	3 years	4 years	5 years
	50	3 years	4 years	5 years	6 years	7 years

*Candidates under 30 must obtain 100 points within any 3-year period for promotion from 1st *kyu* to 1st *dan*; minimum time in grade is 6 months.

prescribed for grade-holders of his age and experience, or he may win the next grade outright candidate's eligibility for promotion, but it can be examined separately at any time after or before the practical requirements are satisfied. Licence holders may enter for examination once in every calendar month.

All important public competitions and official promotion examinations to and within the *dan* degree are designated as point-scoring events. The points recorded and accumulated in a competitor's favour are the valuations given for a win against an opponent of the same or higher grade in the course of the event. The scale of valuation is as follows: win by *ippon* ten points; win by

waza-ari seven points; win by *yuko* five points: win by *koka* at a promotion examination. The inter-relationship of the various factors is shown in the table. three points; win by simple *yuseigachi* one point. At promotion examinations nothing less than *waza-ari* is recorded. Points earned are authenticated and recorded in the score card which is retained by the individual with his judo licence. There is no requirement that a player who has the appropriate number of points for promotion **must** take it; a small minority of competitors prefer to disregard the fact that they have accumulated sufficient points and wait until they manage to win the grade outright at a promotion examination instead. (Similar

considerations apply in respect of the prescribed points target, which is less for thirty year-olds than for those under thirty). Whichever route is used the theory requirement must be satisfied in order to perfect a When promotion is claimed on the basis of sufficient points accumulated it is necessary to show that the candidate has been 'active' at his grade for a certain period of time. Activity is demonstrated either by participation in contest or by proof of teaching and coaching commitments.

Although the examinees at an examination for 1st *dan* and above may have their points recorded for accumulation purposes, the proceedings are conducted on the basis that everyone present is trying to win promotion outright. Every entrant is given two preliminary contests. Those who win both get a chance to take on a three-man line up; those who win one get a further preliminary contest to see whether they can win it and qualify for a line-up too. In order to complete the practical part of the examination the person taking the line must beat each member of it in succession. A 'win' for a candidate aged under thirty means in every case a win by *ippon*. Candidates aged thirty or over may win their preliminary contests for a total of seventeen points (i.e. an *ippon, waza-ari* combination) and defeat the players in the line for a total of twenty-four points (i.e. an *ippon, waza-ari, waza-ari* permutation) in order to qualify.

As with *kyu* grades, the *dan* grades must undergo a theory examination which is cumulative in the sense that it covers everything in the syllabus at and below their present grade. The difference is that failure in the theory part does not deprive a *dan* grade of the points of his contest work, because for him it is a separate examination. At all levels, the demonstration of theory is performed on the move as when *randori* is performed in an easy-going way. Two additional features at *dan* grade examinations are the inclusion of different *katas* in the syllabus and the awarding of marks by the examiners for the standard of demonstration displayed. The available marks correspond with the points given for throws in contest and an overall pass mark (above 60 per cent) must be obtained.

EXAMINATIONS & PROMOTIONS

Belt examinations have always been a fragile area of conflict in the United States. Traditionalists have held that tests are subject to peer review; this is the *yudanshakai* method of promotion. This method does allow for peer review and acceptance by surrounding instructors and athletes of the candidates for advancement. The drawback of this system, at least in the United States model, is that undue local prejudices against or in favor of a candidate for promotion has many times become highly political. This has given rise to a national promotion board which eliminates personal prejudices and allows for only the evaluation of the specific requirements for promotion.

In the United States, divisions are rarely fought by rank categories; *kyu* and *dan* grades all compete within the standard IJF weight divisions. Matching contestants of the same rank is sometimes used in large metropolitan areas. However, insufficient numbers of contestants at each rank level and tradition have caused the almost exclusive use of weight categories in both men's and women's *shiai* divisions. Junior *shiai* divisions are divided by a combination of weight and age factors. *Kata* competition, on the other hand, has utilized rank divisions.

The competition point system in the United States is markedly different from that used in the United Kingdom. Whereas the gross number of points used for *dan* grades is higher in the United Kingdom system, the number of points awarded for scoring is also correspondingly higher. Another difference is the method of awarding contest points. Instead of greater numbers of points for the greater excellence of the score made, greater points are given for scoring against an opponent of higher rank. No consideration is given for how excellent the score was for the win. In converse, less points (even fractional points) are awarded for contesting immediate lower grades. No points are awarded for besting an opponent who holds a grade of three below your own rank.

The United States system of point awarding and divisions does cause many problems.

There are drawbacks for both the novice and advanced players. For beginners, the contesting of high ranking opponents early in their contest judo careers can discourage and eliminate many potential athletes during their early developmental stages. For advanced players, additional matches against lower ranks cause unnecessary exhaustion, little opportunity for high technical play, and no promotion points regardless of the outcome.

In the United States, the concept of a judo license is still new and in the experimental stages. Verification of promotion points is marginal at best. The only real control of promotion is the minimum time in grade factor. The total acceptance of compulsory promotions handled through the various national ranking. bodies is still not universally utilized by many coaches. Furthermore, there are no restrictions to encourage the use of the nationally accepted standards by the judo community as a whole. Junior ranks and senior ranks below *sankyu* are largely issued ' outside of official rank promotion bodies of the United States.

There are shortcomings of any promotional system regardless of design. It has been advocated that the time has arrived to develop a promotional system which will offer certification in many different specialized areas, rather than the single line of promotion of the judo general practitioner. An expanded judo promotional system would take into account far more factors than the current measurement of practical contest ability. Trying to include the noncompetitive provisions within the concept of the all encompassing "Black Belt" has only confused what a rank holder is; and in turn, this has created great animosity among recipients of the many different types of service oriented promotions which are awarded.

Future judo grades should be explicit of the judoka's area of excellence, similar to the specialization of a college or university degree. Black belt grades should be awarded in specific areas of excellence: i.e. *shiai* competitor, *kata* competitor, *shiai* coach, *kata* coach, self-defense instructor, tournament organizer, referee official, administrative leader, etcetera. The distinctions of black belts would reduce the feeling that many judoka have about other persons not having to fulfill the same amount or difficulty of tasks for their promotions.

CHAPTER 21. COMPETITION STRUCTURE

International competition in judo is a comparatively recent phenomenon, a fact which is attributable to three independent factors. In the first place Jigoro Kano was firmly against anything which put winning for its own sake on a pedestal; his views prevailed during his own lifetime and for some years after. Second, the trauma of the Second World War and its aftermath made international co-operation impossible for more than a decade. Third, only token opposition to Japanese supremacy would have been

Ninomiya (Japan) throws Glahn (W. Germany) in the 1973 World Championships with a *makikomi* style *osotogari* on his way to a gold medal: a classic example of the reaping action without which the throw is useless.

possible for many years because of the initial slow growth of judo outside Japan.

Prior to the introduction of judo into the Olympic Games, the major event in the judo calendar was the World Judo Championships, inaugurated in 1956 and held biennially. The first two championships took place in Tokyo and the Japanese overwhelmed the opposition at both events, which were fought at open weight. In 1961 Anton Geesink, a Dutchman aged twenty-seven, weighing 121kg (267 lb) and standing 1.98m tall (6 feet 6 inches) beat Sone, the Japanese reigning world champion, aged thirty-three, weighing 85.5kg, (190lb) and standing 1.78m tall (5 feet 10 inches). His victory broke the Japanese stranglehold on the sport and showed that they were not invincible; it also showed that if international judo were not to be a battle of the giants, weight categories would have to be introduced. As a prelude to competition at different weights in the 1964 Olympics, all international events with effect from 1963 were fought in three categories in addition to an open class. The categories were: lightweight, under 67.5kg; middleweight, under 80kg; heavyweight, over 80kg. These divisions were subdivided in 1966 to produce five categories plus an open, but even this expansion has been superseded by the introduction in 1977 of seven categories plus an open to take account of the increased sophistication of Olympic judo. The weights for senior men competitors are:

60kg and below
65kg and below
71kg and below
78kg and below
86kg and below
95kg and below
over 95kg
all weights

Different weights are used in women's, young men's, boys'

and girls' events and these appear elsewhere in the text as appropriate.

Several methods can be used in judo to find the winner of a championship. The World Championships and the Olympic Games are fought on the basis of a knockout competition with repechage. The names of all competitors are allocated (as drawn) to one or other of two divisions and listed in a column. At each round the number of competitors still in contention reduces by half until only two finalists remain. The table reproduces the draw and results in the heavyweight category at the 1976 Montreal Games. Given that a fixed number of entrants is distributed between two divisions which must symmetrically reduce by half at each stage, the use of byes is obligatory in the first round. The table shows this process in operation.

Eventually two finalists are identified and they meet to decide which of them will take the gold medal. Before this happens a series of repechage contests is held to discover who will win a bronze. The repechage concerns the two groups of players each defeated *en route* by a finalist. The first person to have been eliminated by a given finalist meets the second person to have been so eliminated; the winner meets the third person eliminated and so on until a next-best competitor is found for each finalist. If two bronze medals are on offer they receive one each; if only one is offered they must fight to see who will receive it.

Not infrequently the best players in a category can find themselves drawn in the same division of the table. Only one of them can then go through to the final and a desperate struggle takes place to decide who it will be; the losers have no chance to compete for a

silver medal. Meanwhile the lesser lights have the other division to themselves; they are given the same chance to take the gold, and whoever their losing finalist may be, he will still take a silver. The table demonstrates this weakness to perfection; NOVIKOV eliminated ENDO and REMFRY *en route* to beating NEUREUTHER in the final; ENDO subsequently beat REMFRY in the repechage for third place. This result was tested in the open event when Remfry was drawn with a chance to put the record straight: he beat Neureuther in the second round and went on to take the silver medal; Neureuther went out in the first contest of the repechage and had to be content to rest on his laurels as far as the open was concerned.

The vagaries of the draw can be avoided by seeding established performers in opposite sides of the table and in different halves of the same side, so that they meet closer to the climax of the championship. In Great Britain (and most other countries) this is done as a matter of routine in domestic competitions so as to secure as accurate a result as possible. Moreover, to prevent hardship from a freak result when a competitor has barely warmed up, the BJA conducts the first round of its championship events in pools, with the top two scorers in each going forward into a knockout with repechage.

Pool systems produce the most accurate results because every player fights every other in his group, thus allowing a league of ability to be produced. When pools alone are used in an event, the players can be accurately ranked by correlating their number of wins with the points they have scored. This is an extremely time-consuming process and its principal use is in trials held for a place in the different national squads.

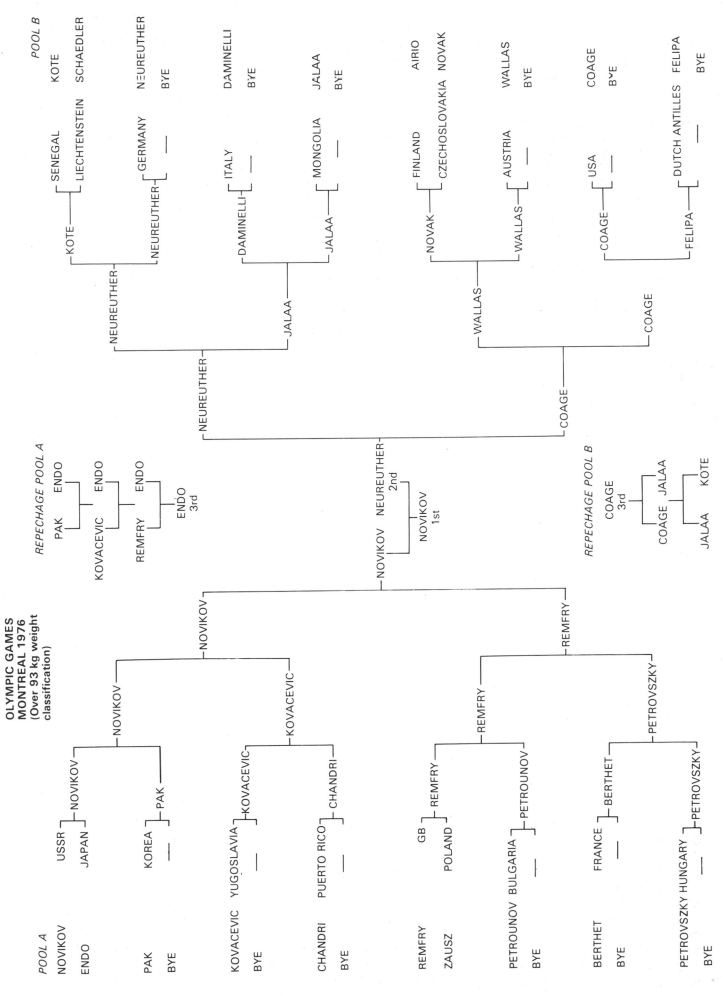

**OLYMPIC GAMES
MONTREAL 1976
(Over 93 kg weight
classification)**

Three, four or five men pools are drawn according to the volume of entries and the top two in each go through to subsequent pools until a final group of four emerges. These four generally become members of the appropriate squad. Should two competitors who have fought each other already be drawn together subsequently, they will not fight again because the result of their first encounter carries forward and is considered decisive.

On a purely domestic basis a wide range of contests is held under the auspices of the BJA. These include national trials, ' national promotion examinations, national *kata* championships, area championships, inter-area team championships, county championships, an All England Championship and many, many more. There is no shortage of opportunity for the player who cannot spare limitless time for judo training but who nevertheless feels able to make a mark for himself; young *judoka* in particular should use the less intense types of competition as a means of gaining experience and attracting the talent scout's eye at an age when their future still lies in front of them.

TOURNAMENTS & GOVERNANCE

Judo tournaments in the United States are sanctioned and/or sponsored by many different organizations. Unlike the United Kingdom, where the BJA holds the IJF franchise over all areas of judo, the United States is more diversely organized.

The United States affiliate to the IJF is the Amateur Athletic Union. The AAU also holds international franchises to several other Olympic and world sports. The role of the AAU in judo is to sanction contests and clinics, to verify the amateur standing of judo athletes, and to select judo teams to represent the United States at the Olympic, World, and Pan American Games.

Certification of judo rank, referees, and coaches is handled by two separate organizations, the United States Judo Association and the United States Judo Federation. Both of these judo organizations are allied bodies of the AAU. The existence of two rank awarding bodies for judo in the United States has been the result of nearly ten years of internal conflict among judo coaches and players.

The current structure of judo in the United States is probably the most sophisticated establishment of a sport's political structure in the world. It is the only example of political democracy in a sport's governing body. The AAU represents the government structure similar to the parliament or congress, the USJA represents progressive judo thought, and the USJF represents traditional judo thought. Within the AAU structure, the USJA and the USJF act as highly-organized political parties working toward the betterment of judo. The competitive nature of these two organizations should provide incentive and initiative for continued improvement. The results of the United States two-party judo system have already expedited acceptance of the IJF contest rules, the IJF weight divisions, and a more equitable distribution of judo rank.

In addition to the AAU's role of general governing body of United States judo, there are several other organizations involved with amateur sports which govern their own national judo championships: the Young Men's Christian Association sanctions a YMCA national judo championship; the National Junior College Athletic Association sanctions their own national championship. The National Collegiate Athletic Association does not officially recognize judo as a senior college sport at the present time.

Preparation must pave the way for success by making winning a feasible proposition. Being prepared for a judo contest simply means going equipped to win. Until the particular requirements of contest judo have been met in training, preparation will be inadequate; therefore the process begins with the anatomy of contest.

Numerous studies have confirmed that six major techniques account for the vast majority of those contests that are decided by *ippon* from a throw. Those techniques are

Minami (Japan) scores with left-handed *seoinage*. Note the distinctive sleeve grip and the direction of effort. The defender failed to get his hand to the mat; even though the thrower is on one knee he had sufficient space in which to turn the opponent over for *ippon*.

seoinage, uchimata, taiotoshi, osotogari, haraigoshi and hanegoshi. The most popular throw varies from year to year but it is invariably one of these six. Prior to the introduction of weight categories, *uchimata* and *osotogari* were all-conquering; along with *taiotoshi* and *seoinage* they were the most prevalent *waza* relied on by All-Japan champions from 1948 to 1960. Every champion used one or more of them as his *tokuiwaza* (most favoured technique).

Following the introduction of weight classes, a detailed Japanese study published in 1966 examined the *tokuiwaza* of 471 students aged between fifteen and eighteen. The students ranged between 1st *dan* and 3rd *dan* and can be considered representative of future champions of that time. None of the big six throws suited both short and tall players. *Uchimata* was the tall students' throw *par excellence*; lightweights had *seoinage* virtually to themselves, and the heavier weights tended to monopolize *osotogari*. *Taiotoshi*,

---

Photo 1—An effective combination sequence during the 1975 World Championships. Reissman (E. Germany) attacked Farrow (Canada) with a powerful left-handed *seoinage*. Farrow responds by sinking his hips and propping rigidly against the throw.

haraigoshi and *hanegoshi* were used at all weights; taller players at a given weight favoured *haraigoshi*, whereas the other two throws were more popular with stocky, squarely-built contestants.

Reference to the Montreal Olympic statistics shows that these results are reproduced internationally. *Seoinage* was the principal scorer in the light

Photo 2—The weakness of the defence is exposed as Reissman fixes his opponent's position momentarily . . .

and light-middle weight categories; *uchimata* was the most successful throw at middleweight and *osotogari* and *taiotoshi* together were the principal scorers at light-heavy and heavy. The general pattern of the open weight All Japan Championships from 1948 to 1960 was also confirmed by the fact that *seoinage, uchimata* and *taiotoshi* figured prominently in every category.

The inference from these statistics is that an effective

repertoire must include a selection of these big throws. *Uchimata* suits the long-limbed player; those with a low centre of gravity can exploit *seoinage*; heavier weights can win with *osotogari.* At every weight, taller than average men show *haraigoshi* to good advantage, those of medium height for their weight find *taiotoshi* and *hanegoshi* effective. Since of course the relative height of two contestants varies, every player should develop throws

117

for situations in which he is the taller and the shorter of two.

Having ensured that the repertoire includes statistically relevant throws, the next stage is to build a range of complementary moves. It is no good being one-sided and/or unidirectional. There must be a big throw on both sides and a supporting throw in the opposite direction. Thus: a long-limbed player may take up *uchimata*. He then either polishes the same throw on the other side or develops another

such as *haraigoshi;* in that case his back-up throw to the rear might be *kouchigari* or *ouchigari,* again capable of execution on either side.

Not every throw is a winner, particularly if the attacker is a player who is apprehensive of going into *katame waza*. Fear of failing robs an attack of sincerity and in this way a lack of *katame waza* preparation can undo conscientious training in *nage waza*. At present a good groundwork specialist can win far beyond his standing

capabilities by capitalizing on the general weakness in *katame waza*. It seems that many players regard groundwork as less skilful than standing judo. In fact the opposite is true; one false move on the ground is usually decisive for *ippon*, which is not often the case in standing judo. Accordingly, there must be equal emphasis in contest training on both branches of mat work. This

Photo 3—. . .before delivering *ouchigari* on the other side for a follow-up to the rear.

lends variety to training and gives confidence while competing.

Success in high-level contest depends on an ability to make use of reaction. An opponent is unlikely to make a mistake voluntarily, so he must be coaxed into error. A winner is an opportunist making his own opportunities and this is why a match has all the subtlety of a chess game.

Use of reactions begins with matters of grip. Push a man and he tends to push back; pull him and he tends to pull away; press him down on one side and he will rise up. These are simple reactions which can be relied on against average players. Beyond that, greater sophistication is required. A committed contest man begins with an idea of the mutual body positioning helpful for a given attack; he then assesses how reaction to grip might bring about that positioning. For example *kosotogari* might be engineered as follows: catch hold of the opponent's right sleeve at the elbow; pass the grip over to your own right hand and step in and past the arm; immediately grasp his· jacket at the nape of the neck with your free left hand and draw his body weight onto his right leg; make a strong attack with *kosotogari* against his supporting side.

Quite apart from making an opening for a specific throw, grip work can distract an opponent, rendering him vulnerable to whatever attack might then be appropriate. As a general fault players expect to have a hold in order to fight. They are unable to get going until they have one and find it distressing to be denied. So.be it. Deny them a familiar hand

A feint to the opponent's front can be rapidly developed into this attack to the rear, provided that the support leg is correctly placed at the outset. Here, Tripet (France) elegantly disposes of a Russian competitor for *ippon*.

Loosening-up exercises prior to the big event.

hold. In striving for a grip they can be led into a throw. Thus, withdrawing the lapel as an opponent reaches for it can make him over-reach. Once his weight is over his advanced foot he should be quickly gripped and thrown over it with *taiotishi.*

Reaction comes to the fore when a feint is used to induce the positioning for a favoured attack. An example of this occurs when *osotogari* is switched at the crucial moment into *hizaguruma* on the other side: by bracing against the expected rear throw the opponent has made his posture weak to the front. Similarly, an attack with *taiotoshi* made from one side of the opponent as if to reach across him encourages him to brace backwards; by quickly

switching the attacking leg from front to rear he can be thrown onto his back with *kosotogari* or *kosotogake.* As this is a game of bluff and double bluff, it is as well to be capable of finishing with either of the coupled throws; an expected feint that never was is effective in its own right.

A further stage of reaction is employed in *renrakuwaza* (combination techniques). Here there is no feint; the first throw in a series of two or more is calculated to score, failing which it will provide an opening for the second throw, and so on. Take the example of a *kouchigari* attack. Should it fail the opponent will withdraw the leg attacked in order to maintain balance. There is an opportunity to follow up with *taiotoshi* or *seoinage* on the

same side, depending on how much space has been created.

Simply plant the attacking foot where it stood when the *kouchigari* failed and spin round on it for the follow-up throw to the front. If the follow-up fails, a further *ouchigari* on the other side should at least score a knock-down. Link techniques are an essential part of contest preparation and great care should be taken to develop fluency in a variety of sequences.

In *randori* there is give and take, but in contest all points must be fought for. A player is not beaten by a throw until he has been put to the mat with impetus; defensive moves which would be misplaced in

skill training must therefore be used to prevent defeat whenever possible. As always the best defence is counter-attack, and counters should be worked out for all the major throws (the *gonosenno-kata* is helpful here). When a counter is impractical something more coarse is called for; such as thrusting the hips forward and snatching back the opponent's grip on the jacket; or swamping his attack by steam-rolling straight through it. If this fails and there is a risk of being toppled, wriggle while being thrown and try to turn away before impact; or get an arm to the mat and push off with it; or lever out from the opponent's body in an attempt to counterbalance his effort with bodyweight. Never think 'Oh, I'm being thrown',

and wait for the impact. Go for a strangle or armlock against the thrower on the assumption that the contest will continue on the ground; and in case things go badly on the ground, be ready with methods of escape and counterattack from all the orthodox holds. An agile defender is always harder to beat than a static one.

A partial aspect of preparation for winning is the ability to weigh in at the correct weight on the day. It is rarely possible to change categories after entering. With the introduction of narrower ranges for each category there is now a temptation for every player to cut weight and drop down a class. If the weight can be shed without serious inconvenience then it should be lost; on the other hand starvation down to

British Olympic medallists Brian Jacks 6th Dan (left) and Dave Starbrook 5th Dan line up for a team contest. Every player experiences tension before competing but . . .

an unnatural weight is incompatible with efficient performance. A fully fit player can barely spare 3kg fluctuation between events, but a less fit person has more leeway. As a rough guide, there is probably enough surplus weight to allow a drop in category if folds of fat more than 26mm thick can be pinched up with finger and thumb from around the waistline.

When weight is to be lost, it is essential to plan for reduction at the rate of 500gm to 1 kg per week. An increase in the rate of exercise coupled with a decrease in the intake of

. . . it's worth it in the end.

calories will have the desired effect. What is not acceptable is a crash diet in the last week before an event, culminating in attempts to sweat off vital body fluids on the day in order to get past the scales. The practise is irresponsible even though a few well-known competitors do make a habit of it. Performance must suffer because crash dieting succeeds by dehydration achieved at the expense of stored energy. Food and drink taken after the weigh-in is of no assistance because of the slow rate of metabolism within the body and is counter-productive in that blood necessary for oxygen transport to the muscles is diverted to the alimentary tract.

The level of stored energy reflects the endurance element of training. Those who have no trouble making their weight may find a technique of dietary manipulation known as carbohydrate loading useful for temporarily increasing their stores of muscle glycogen. Although it is used regularly in other endurance sports, there is no record so far of its use in judo training. The technique is employed during the last week before an event. For the first three days the athlete trains hard on a diet almost exclusively composed of fats and protein; this exhausts his stores of muscle glycogen. In the three days immediately before the event, however, he switches to a high carbohydrate diet in conjunction with only a low level of training activity. This induces the body to over-react by increasing its store of glycogen, and both endurance and rate of work benefit accordingly.

Fine tuning for a competition covers approximately four weeks for a player who is already fit. This reflects the biological reality that bodily condition is at any given time a measure of what has gone on during the preceding month. The aim is overhaul and not test to destruction; enough work to present a well-oiled machine at the mat on the day and no more. The emphasis is on enjoyable workouts coupled with exertion at maintenance level. Confidence-building routines ought to replace hard-fought trials of skill and, since sleep cannot be stored or replaced, adequate rest must be taken. A player who is not fully fit must reckon on at least a two-month run up to an important event, the first month to be spent on hard training, the second as outlined above.

Fixed ideas belong in wooden brains, and the trouble with a word like strategy is that it encourages belief in fixed ideas. 'Strategy' is a word with many shades of meaning, all of which imply that a player can take a master plan to the mat with him and win on the strength of it. The swordsman and zen master Odagiri Ichiun had no doubt that strategy was a delusion which cluttered up the reality of a confrontation. In his book *The Demonstration of Throws,* Trevor Leggett expands the proposition as follows: 'Techniques which are mechanically perfect will nevertheless fail if the opponent is expecting them, in other words if they are strategically ineffective.' This statement shows that strategy develops out of the opponent's state of readiness, not out of a pre-determined plan of action.

Judo embodies the only relevant strategy–that of *ju* (see Chapter 2) – and the task in every situation is to allow it to operate. In a self-defence situation it is reasonably easy to use an attacker's aggression against him. A contest between equals is altogether different. The object of the exercise is to prove the existence of weakness in the opponent's movements. Every attack poses a question which demands an answer from him; when he can no longer reply he is beaten. Searching out his weaknesses means taking his measure as he fights; each attack must be exploratory, and it is not good enough to slog away with the same set piece. Factors of distance speed and direction should be varied to produce a different question every time. As Trevor Leggett wrote:

'Remember that, as one teacher told me, you are trying to outwit not the opponent's brain but his bodily reactions. In contest he has no time to think but relies on the reactions of the body as trained in Judo.

''And the body (added the teacher) is quite a stupid thing!'' *

Although the variables of contest militate against preconceived strategy, the constant features of a competition can and should be dealt with. Matters arising after the weigh-in are primarily psychological. The exception is that of servicing the body during the day. Successful participation in an event is always tiring. Energy must be maintained, and after prolonged exertion the body's water and mineral salts need to be replenished. The problem calls for a solution during and after hard judo, but not before (except in the case of a player who has had to diet in order to

The transition from standing judo to groundwork can occur unexpectedly. Here, Adams (Great Britain) snatches an armlock as his opponent stumbles to his knees.

* (The Demonstration of Throws, T P Leggett, Foulsham)

compete). The reason for pointing this out is that preventive energization in anticipation may do more harm than good. Quick-energy foods and drinks produce an immediate increase in blood sugar; a correspondingly increased insulin reaction follows, designed to promote rapid absorption. In due course this can produce an excessive fall in blood glucose levels with the unpleasant sequel of a hypoglycaemic 'crash'.

Several proprietary brands of drink are available for servicing the body during a competition. None are particularly cheap, none improve skill and none can make energy available instantaneously. They do, however, offer good replacement of depleted minerals, thus aiding recovery, and they do supply carbohydrate in a readily-assimilated form. As a cheaper alternative, bearing

Photo 1—Response to attack Take-down. Iwata (Japan) makes a major attack with right-handed *seoinage.* Consider the thrower in isolation and notice his left-hand grip, the curl of his right wrist and the position of his head. A *kiai* is frozen on his lips. Had the thrower managed to insert his right arm under the defender's arm, he would have dropped and thrown well.

in mind that fluid must be replaced somehow, the reader might like to consider the preparation suggested by a British

Photo 2—However, imagine a straight line between the thrower's feet; Scott (Ireland) scoops his attacker's legs from behind by rotating his hips and upper body, and takes the thrower backwards over the imaginary line.

newspaper *(The Sunday Times)* in 1977. Dilute a pure fruit juice base with an equal amount of water; add a pinch of table salt (not enough to alter the taste) and glucose (not sugar) in the proportion of one heaped dessert spoon to every 300 ml.

Any fruit juice is suitable according to taste.

Nervousness tends to sap energy and it is unwise to get hot and bothered before going on to the mat. Everyone feels some nervousness before a contest; that is a fact. Champion athletes have been known to vomit with anticipation and then break a world record. Accept that fact, but do not wallow in it. Nothing is more certain than that nervousness will vanish once

you are on the mat, and it would be ludicrous to allow months of training to disappear in a slush of self-indulgent emotion beforehand. Just go about your business. If idle chatter and silly jokes irritate you, go and sit quietly on your own somewhere. Read a book, watch the contests, or go to sleep if you prefer. Keep warm; make sure that you have loosened up completely, but do not go too far in warming up, a

125

mock sweat represents that much wasted energy.

When called to the mat walk boldly forward, bow to the referee, bow to the opponent and wait for the command *hajime.* When it comes go smoothly into action. Take hold of your man and throw him off the very ground he stands on.

Be certain that if once he stumbles, he will not rise to his feet again except as a beaten contestant. Do your utmost to overawe him from the outset: never let him settle into a congenial pace; move consciously not haphazardly; always keep your objective in mind. It is no part of your function to predict the outcome; you have a job to do and telling yourself how difficult or easy it is will not get it done. Your job is to prove that you can turn his movements to your own advantage, so let that happen by generating movement.

The word 'tactic' is interpreted by some players as meaning 'antics and tricks'. Experienced referees know enough to stamp on players who waste time, but there nevertheless remains sufficient scope for manoeuvre within the rules to

Photo 1—Response to attack Snatch back the grip; crash through the attack. Han Suk Lee (Korea) applies a devastating *uchimata* but loses upper body control as Coche (France) snatches his right arm free.

encourage deviousness. This is the result of a detailed rulebook; 'what is not prohibited is not an infringement' or so the argument goes. Deviousness takes many forms, some more culpable than others, such as: folding the right side of the jacket well across,

Photo 2—Even without the vital sleeve grip, the thrower lifts Coche clear of the mat. Coche spreads his legs to maintain balance and begins to power his left hip forwards through the attack.

and on top of, the left side in the knowledge that it will soon be pulled out of the belt; tying bandages loosely so that they come undone; rasping an unshaven chin against the opponent's skin during groundwork; kneeling on the opponent's thigh muscle in order to get past his legs or (at the back of the thigh) in order to turn him off his stomach; browbeating the referee into a false *ippon* by jumping for joy as

though the score was a foregone conclusion. The view that 'as long as an opponent is beaten within the letter of the rules, *how* does not matter' is not in the true spirit of judo. Try always to win because you deserve to.

Much the same considerations govern tactics as strategy: the contest must be played by ear. There is a difference, in that recurring situations can be thought out in advance on the basis that statistically they are

likely to be encountered from time to time. No strategy can make a situation occur, but a tactical advantage can be taken if it does. The most frequent advantage to be gained is at the expense of an opponent who has backed into a corner of the mat. He cannot step backwards for fear of a penalty. Knowing that, a good contest man will have rehearsed the situation a hundred times over in training so that he can exploit the inevitable step forward.

Another advantage to be gained is at the expense of an opponent with an oxygen debt (see Chapter 26). The moment you hear him overbreathing, step up the pace in standing work or put your bodyweight over his chest in groundwork.

Against an opponent who struggles desperately to avoid groundwork, the right tactic is to take the contest to the floor because he has advertised his weakness in that department. Against an opponent who hugs the edge of the mat or who tends to move sideways, *okuriashiharai,* the big ankle technique, is a promising tactic. As a general ploy, try to draw the opponent's head and shoulders on to the perpendicular running through your own centre of gravity when attacking with a big body throw;

Photo 3—With one foot down the defender gets clear of the throw and bears down on the thrower.

where the head has gone the body will usually follow.

Needless to say, contest is the wrong time to examine the motive for entering competitive judo. Psychologists believe that the principal limitation on performance in any athlete is that imposed by personality; the physical boundary is never reached. It is certainly true that

Photo 4—In less than 1 second the thrower crumbles and his attack is neutralized.

judo champions are not squeamish about the sweat and grind of hard contest; not everyone has that type of personality and it is instructive to discover what constitutes the champions' outlook. The Japanese popularly refer to a wrestler by the name of O-Nami (great waves). He is said to have become All Japan champion in days of yore after meditating on the theme of a surging sea. The ebb and flow of tidal energy

swept away the doubts in his mind, enabling him to engulf his rivals on the mat. In similar vein, it is said of Angelo Parisi (until recently a member of the British team) that his phenomenal success stemmed from a vision he maintained in which he possessed all the power of a comic strip hero.

The interesting feature of both anecdotes is that neither champion set out to work up a hatred for his opponents. Such

aggressiveness as there was, was directed at themselves: they rigorously eliminated all personal considerations in favour of impersonal power. There is nothing in this type of 'aggression' amounting to personal violence; the opponent loses at the hands of a *judoka* functioning as executioner. The winner is neither sad nor glad until the deed is done.

For some people the necessary detachment is an impossibility. This does not mean that they will never have

success; it only means that they will never enjoy extraordinary success. The same emotional involvement that robs them of detachment will also prevent them from training in disregard of personal comfort and convenience; without that commitment there can be no Olympic medal. Even though success breeds success, champions still have their crises. Losing comes hard to a player who has known only increasing success. And yet it is inevitable in the long run.

Having tumbled Inman (Great Britain) with *taiotoshi* to the left, Starbrook (Great Britain) follows up immediately with a strong *kesagatame.*

Without the maturity to appreciate that winning is a privilege, a player can lose the necessary positive outlook on competition. he begins to see defeat as a personal slander instead of a fortune of war. Once demoralized, there will follow a spiral of failure. Excuses can always be made but a touch of humility is the only real antidote.

There are increasing opportunities for women to make their mark in competition judo. Christine Wildman 4th Dan (right) closes on her opponent during the 1974 British Open Championships.

In Japanese society the traditional role of women required that they accept male dominance without question. Whatever was unthinkable to the Japanese male was thus unthinkable to the Japanese female, and so womanhood existed as men understood it to be. Ju-jutsu was a martial art which fostered the 'male' virtues of strength, endurance and competitiveness; although not wholly unknown, lady ju-jutsuka were a great rarity. Judo on the other hand was conceived as an education for life, and once Kano had so described it there was no longer any logical reason why women should be excluded. Surprisingly, misgivings about female involvement persisted, and it was not until 1923 that Kano formally established a women's division of the Kodokan.

As pressure built up for the establishment of a women's judo section, Kano gave much thought to the manner in which such a section would learn the art. He ruled out contest work on the ground that, despite their lack of physical strength, the will to win would lead women into forceful judo. The prospect of women appearing rough and ungainly on the mat troubled him and ultimately led him to the conclusion that women's judo should comprise *kata,* light *randori* and self-defence exercises. The · prescribed *kata* for women was *junokata,* even though it had been a *kata* for high-grade men since its adoption at the Kodokan in 1887 and was considered difficult to perform correctly. In simplifying judo for women in this way Kano had not the slightest intention of deprecating their ability to learn; in fact he insisted that the best instructors should teach the women members and was fond of telling people that the methods used developed skill in true judo. Nevertheless, the undeniable criticism is that his judgement could not but reflect a cultural bias against full involvement by women in a man's sport. The judgement of those women who learned under him was similarly biased and the task of emancipating women's judo therefore fell on lady *judoka* in the western hemisphere.

The thrust behind women's judo in Europe has come from British players. In 1958 there were less than ten women *dan* grade holders practising in British clubs, but by 1976 the number had reached 303 (including five 4th *dans*) and is still growing. This expansion has taken place against a background of reassessment of the conventional Japanese approach resulting ultimately in its rejection. What began as a national initiative soon became a continental initiative as European women demonstrated their enthusiasm for international contests. Thereafter the IJF itself set the pace by declaring in November 1974 that: 'If Women's Judo Championships are conducted successfully by at least three Continental Unions the IJF will duly consider sponsoring World

Women's Judo Championships and also including Women's Judo Championships in the Olympic Games. The target date for conducting such Women's Judo Championships will be 1980.' It seems unlikely that a women's event will be included in the Moscow Olympic Games in 1980, but there is every possibility, now that the idea is acceptable in principle, that female readers of this book will find themselves vying for a place in an Olympic team by 1984.

Reassessment of the Japanese model was piecemeal. Until 1961 few people saw any need to accord separate status to women; they practised alongside men at club level and were humoured as brave souls in a man's world. Dame Enid Russell-Smith (the first woman outside Japan to reach 3rd *dan*) occupied an influential position as editor of the Budokwai *Quarterly Bulletin,* but there was barely any voice in women's judo for her to put before the readership. Then, in 1961, a BJA sub-committee was formed to take in hand the growth and betterment of women's judo in the UK. A women's syllabus was introduced and the Japanese (American also) custom of wearing the appropriate colour belt with a white stripe along its length was adopted. This was intended to show parity of grade with men in a sister species of grades; since the wearing of striped belts became optional in 1972, the custom has largely been abandoned in favour of plain colour designation.

The introduction of competition for women marked the point of divergence with Japanese orthodoxy. The first event in Britain was a team contest and *kata* championship held at Liverpool University in 1966. It was a private event because it was generally thought that women's judo did not justify an audience. With hindsight this can be seen as expressing one of the classic misassumptions that has bedevilled judo. The

misassumption is that judo is a man's sport. It is not a man's sport any more than running or swimming. That being so, there is no warrant for sayng that women distract attention from the 'right' impression being created by men. Later, in 1971, the first British Open Individual Championship was held and it drew players from West Germany and observers from the Netherlands; held annually ever since, this has become a major international event which now attracts competitors from Australia, New Zealand and North America, as well as from Europe. Following a trial tournament in 1974, a permanent annual European Championship for women has been established and it, too, is one of the prestige events in women's judo.

The European competition structure has thrown up some interesting trends. British women have dominated in international matches at home and abroad as a consequence of their early progressive attitude to contest judo. The opposition is quickly closing on them, however, partly because of the support given them by ex-international male players. As yet the Eastern Socialist bloc has declined to take part, but they will undoubtedly be a force to reckon with in due course when their 'sports machine' grinds into action, especially in the heavier weight categories in which there is at present a shortage of top-class competitors.

Women's judo in the United States has in many ways developed similarly to its counterpart in the United Kingdom. Some recent accomplishments include a single standard of promotion for both women and men, women's tournaments for both *shiai* and *kata,* and women participants at the national planning level.

The United States partici-pation in the British Women's Open during 1976 and 1977

Groundwork is a strenuous pastime. The jujigatame sought by the burly Russian above has been applied by the young lady below—without co-operation in either case.

has adequately demonstrated that the United States women are in a significantly dominant place in major international competition. The same contest excellence was also shown at the First Pan American Women's Championship held in 1977. The ability of the United States women's team to win a majority of awards at these three events is in great contrast to the poor showing that United States men's teams have made in international competition.

The United States men's teams have never ranked higher than twentieth place in world judo. This poorer showing of the men's teams versus the women's teams is caused by many factors. The use of domestic AAU contest rules, which deviated drastically from IJF contest rules, is one major reason why United States men's teams have fallen behind: many years of judo play under different rules has defeated many American judo players long before they ever stepped on the international contest mat.

United States women on the other hand are better prepared for international competition, because they have played domestically for many years under current IJF contest rules. Good preparation and early international successes have caused positive ego development among American women *judoka.*

Another reason for the gap between American men and women in world judo competition is the greater range of professional sports offered to men, which attract many of the nation's best male athletes. The number of professional women's sports are decidedly fewer, therefore, judo has been able to attract some of the better women athletes in the country.

There is no doubt that fair competition requires the separation of men from women in contest, even in the weights

are roughly equal. The strength of each sex is not faithfully represented by bodyweight; at any given weight a man possesses a greater proportion of muscle than a woman. In non-contact sports such as swimming, cycling and track athletics, the records show that women can now reach 91 per cent of male performance compared with 88 per cent thirty years ago. Better training methods have obviously increased woman's strength. Nevertheless, in judo men and woman could not compete on equal terms unless competitors could be matched solely by reference to their maximum available strength; failing that the only alternative is single-sex competition in weight categories as at present.

The weight categories in use for women are as follows:
SENIOR WOMEN (age 16 and over)
48kg and below
52kg and below
56kg and below
61kg and below
66kg and below
72kg and below
Over 72kg
All weights: Open
YOUNG WOMEN
44kg and below
48kg and below
52kg and below
56kg and below
60kg and below
65kg and below
Over 65kg
All weights : Open
SCHOOLGIRLS
32kg and below
36kg and below
40kg and below
44kg and below
48kg and below
52kg and below
56kg and below
60kg and below
65kg and below
Over 65kg
All weights : Open

Top women players consider these categories fair, with the possible exception of the 'Over

72kg class; this has attracted some imposing physiques in recent years, and if World and Olympic competition continue the trend it may become necessary to introduce a further division at about 86kg.

A woman's biological (though not necessarily social) estate in life is motherhood. She is naturally disposed towards early sexual maturity, periodic cycles of ovulation and the immediate management of any pregnancy she undergoes. As with all the factors already identified, women's judo must take these matters into account at the organizational level; none of them dictates that women should train differently for judo from men, though.

Early maturity has important implications for women's judo. On the mat, young women of sixteen compete to good advantage against older players. In 1975 the average age of the British senior women's squad was twenty-five; in 1977 it was twenty-one, soon it will be nineteen. This means that candidates for the squad must be in the forefront while still at school in order to get the right grounding in judo. The snag is that off the mat the bright prospects may have to choose between judo or a career at a crucial juncture; because men reach the top later in life, circumstances often decide the issue for them. The choice is further complicated by the fact that, with a few exceptions, women are finished with international competition by the time they are twenty-six. It is not a coincidence that the top British women are intelligent people with professions that are compatible with judo. A short contest career with nothing to follow is a serious undertaking.

Menstruation produces physiological disturbances the

Adams (Great Britain) performs a *makikomi* style *uchimata;* total commitment coupled with a perfect leg action, though not quite enough upper-body control.

effects of which vary enormously from person to person. Researchers are not certain whether the varying effects are a result of differing symptoms or differing tolerance thereof. The capacity to train hard for a sport implies a good tolerance of discomfort and the evidence indicates that physically active women cope well with their periods. The onset of a period need not be bad news: judo is a good outlet for pre-menstrual aggression and a number of athletes actually perform better at that time of the month. Organizational sympathy is required, however, with regard to the weight gain which for some women precedes the onset of a period. This can be as much as 2kg or 3kg; it can be alleviated by the use of diuretics under medical supervision, and a competitor who might not otherwise make her weight is advised to consult her doctor in advance of the event.

The dedication required of a lady champion is no less than that required of a male champion. Three evenings a week on the mat is a minimum, and that must be supplemented by running, circuit-training or weight-training on a daily basis. For contest training and *randori* the best partners are adolescent male 1st *kyus* aged between sixteen and twenty; adult men in general (and adult male beginners in particular) must be avoided for these purposes unless they are positively known to be capable of productive practice. A woman who is going to compete must also be able to turn on the necessary aggression as part of her emotional make-up. She must switch off from her surroundings and become single-minded in her will to win. 'Aggression' does not mean disregarding an opponent's physical safety, but it does require a self-assertiveness without which technical

competence is insufficient to nurture a champion. In Great Britain at present six weekends a year are set aside for national squad training sessions, with a full programme of competitions in addition. There are talented women willing to go through with this training, but not in great numbers. Young women who are interested in trying have, perhaps, an even better chance of realising their ambition than young men.

Not everyone wishes to be a champion and most of the women who regularly slip into a leotard and *judogi* do so because judo is a source of enjoyment for them. The exercise is comprehensive, the sport is safe and it is a satisfying emotional outlet. Dame Enid Russell-Smith began judo in 1937 at the age of thirty-four and received a 4th *dan* in 1971; more women of every age should ask themselves whether they could not do the same.

CHAPTER 25. JUNIOR JUDO

The most progressive area of modern judo is that devoted to junior judo. When the sport was adopted at Olympic level, the membership of the BJA bulged at the bottom end of the age range, a response which augurs well for the future. As a result, whereas yesterday's champions may not have taken up judo until they were twenty, today's hopes lie with promising young players who are in the sport as young as twelve or thirteen. Talent-spotting is a special interest for coaches and administrators, and a network of suitable competitions undreamt of ten years ago exists to identify young people of ability. It would nevertheless be wrong to assume that official interest centres only on the hot-house plants who might become champions. Junior judo is valuable in its own right, whatever the level of achievement from person to person. It possesses the ideal

combination of qualities: speed, agility and imagination, so often lacking in adult judo; and it serves to develop personal characteristics worth having in the world outside school.

The lowest practical age for beginning judo is about seven or eight. Below that age a child has insufficient strength and co-ordination to permit full participation. In many clubs the children's classes are mixed until the children approach puberty; thereafter it is usual for the girls to join the women's section and for the older boys to be segregated from their younger counterparts in junior practice sessions. in every class the instructor takes pains to ensure that within reasonable limits the pupils are matched by height and weight.

Such is the extent of interest in judo for young people that many schools include the sport in their curriculum. Local education authorities in London maintain

full-time judo instructors and a number of public schools offer judo to the exclusion of traditional sports like boxing and rugby football. The British Schools Judo Association (BSJA) forms a special division within the judo administration in Britain and it exists to co-ordinate and develop judo in schools; the Association enjoys sizeable support and claims to be the only organization of its kind in the world. It is possible that in the future the growth of judo in schools will bear fruit in the universities and that they will become strongholds of judo as in Japan. The British Universities Judo Association (BUJA) is part of the BJA and aims to build on the foundations of judo knowledge possessed by its student members. Most students are at present the products of

Concentration is required at all levels of competition.

BJA member clubs rather than of the schools themselves. With a greater emphasis on school-based judo, the annual university intake would contain a greater number of experienced players. Better use could then be made of the unique training opportunities afforded by university life.

In Europe the term 'junior' is somewhat confusing in as much as it refers to three separate age categories according to context. The BJA treats boys and girls aged eight to fifteen as juniors for both competition and promotion purposes unless they themselves, on the advice of their instructors, opt out of the concession in order to enter senior promotion examinations. Since the introduction of an eighteen-grade structure for juniors this has rarely been considered desirable. For competition purposes the EJU recognizes two further classes of young player, 'junior' (aged eighteen to twenty) and 'espoir' (young hopeful, aged sixteen to eighteen), and stages a championship for each every year. A different scheme of weight categories applies to competition in each of the three age bands.

Official competitions for schoolboys use the following weight categories:
30kg and below
35kg and below
40kg and below
45kg and below
50kg and below
55kg and below
60kg and below
65kg and below
70kg and below
Over 70kg
Those in use for young women and schoolgirls are shown in Chapter 24.

Events for senior men and women (i.e. members of the BJA aged sixteen and over) use the weights shown in Chapters 21 (men) and 24 (women) unless the competition is especially designated a 'young men's' event. In that case the following categories apply:

Comparative left-handed *taiotoshi:* Starbrook (Great Britain) powers his opponent over with a strong upper body action but fails to score *ippon* from the throw. The contest continued on the ground where Starbrook won with *kesagatame.* Below, Sato (Japan) places his legs superbly. The absolute ideal is Starbrook's upper body movement combined with Sato's leg action.

YOUNG MEN (ESPOIR)
53kg and below
57kg and below
62kg and below
68kg and below
75kg and below
83kg and below
Over 83kg

Junior 18 – 20
60kg and below
65kg and below
71kg and below
78kg and below
86kg and below

95kg and below
Over 95kg
There are no corresponding 'young women's' categories.

The pattern of promotion examinations for juniors follows the broad outline of senior examinations (see Chapter 20), although a wholly different grade structure is used. The grades are known as *mon* (threshold) grades; their identification is as follows:

1st *mon* white + one red bar

2nd *mon*	white + two red bars
3rd *mon*	white + three red bars
4th *mon*	yellow + one red bar
5th *mon*	yellow + two red bars
6th *mon*	yellow + three red bars
7th *mon*	orange + one red bar
8th *mon*	orange + two red bars
9th *mon*	orange + three red bars
10th *mon*	green + one red bar
11th *mon*	green + two red bars
12th *mon*	green + three red bars
13th *mon*	blue + one red bar
14th *mon*	blue + two red bars
15th *mon*	blue + three red bars
16th *mon*	brown + one red bar
17th *mon*	brown + two red bars
18th *mon*	brown + three red bars

Juniors may enter promotion examinations once every three calendar months. The examiner has a discretion as to whether the contests fought will be for a single *ippon* or for the best of three *ippons*. Candidates up to and including 15th *mon* are given a minimum of two contests of two or three minutes each according to age. This increases to three contests in the case of persons holding 16th and 17th *mon*. Positive efforts are made to pit children of the same size weight and age against one another wherever possible.

It is most important for juniors to realize that one or two wins do not automatically justify promotion. Everything depends on the examiners' final recommendations and he is charged with the responsibility for ensuring that the standard of the highest *mon* grades approximates with that of a senior 2nd or 1st *kyu*. When formerly there were fewer *mon* grades to be won, the junior grades were not strictly earned as *kyu* grade equivalents. Now *mon* grades of 6th *mon* and above translate into provisional

kyu grades when the holder reaches sixteen years of age. The scale of conversion is as follows:

6th *mon*	provisional 9th *kyu*
7th, 8th *mon*	provisional 8th *kyu*
9th *mon*	provisional 7th *kyu*
10th, 11th *mon*	provisional 6th *kyu*
12th *mon*	provisional 5th *kyu*
13th, 14th *mon*	provisional 4th *kyu*
15th *mon*	provisional 3rd *kyu*
16th, 17th *mon*	provisional 2nd *kyu*
18th *mon*	provisional 1st *kyu*

The *kyu* grade entitlement is in every case subject to formal recognition at a senior promotion examination. The examiner need not, having assessed a candidate's performance, award the full equivalent senior grade if he feels that a lower *kyu* grade is more appropriate.

The transition from a junior to senior training sessions can be a difficult experience. From being high in the junior hierarchy, a young player moves on to the lower rungs of the senior hierarchy; without the necessary maturity to accept the new status, there is a danger that he or she will be lost to the sport. The best way to tackle this problem is undoubtedly to soften the blow by selecting suitable juniors, at the first opportunity, to stay behind and practice with seniors for twenty minutes or half an hour some time before they reach the age of sixteen and have to be pushed out of the junior class. Sessions spent with the seniors provide an excellent opportunity for juniors to familiarize themselves with *kansetsuwaza* and *shimewaza*. Under the present rules such techniques are forbidden in junior competition. Juniors have never been prevented from practising or,

more importantly, having these techniques practised on them; unfortunately the prohibition against using these *waza* in contest has been misinterpreted with the result that too many juniors are ill-prepared for their first experience of adult judo. *Provided that qualified instructors are present,* juniors pre-selected for adult classes should be encouraged to learn what are, in fact, important and effective contest techniques.

Other difficulties arise from the physical and social implications of being a teenager. Increased weight and rapid growth can interfere dramatically with the timing of a *tokuiwaza* and lead to the frustration of appearing clumsy on the mat. The disadvantage of being seventeen and having to fight a physically mature adult in groundwork can create a permanent aversion to *katamewaza* in which strength can really be made to count. The additional pressures of study, leisure, work, girl (boy) friends and other sports are all liable to increase to a point at which they encroach upon time earmarked for judo unless a conscious effort is made to prevent that happening. There is, of course, no magic solution to any of these problems. In the final analysis they reduce to a test of motivation for which the only answer is dogged determination. However, dogged determination is the paramount requirement for any champion and since the journey to championship honours begins with the first step, adolescence is as good a time as any to develop the right qualities.

It is useful to understand the factors which influence the way a training programme is put together before turning to the specific needs of judo. This chapter is a collection of relevant explanations; the full terminology has been used for the sake of accuracy but the reader is advised not to be put off by it: long words are not essential to insight.

An elementary topic to begin with is the calorie as a measurement of energy. Raising the temperature of 1kg of water by 1 degree Centigrade consumes 1 calorie of energy applied regardless of the form that energy took. Thus, any amount of energy can be expressed in calories according to the quantity of water it could notionally heat through 1 degree Centigrade. The human energy requirement depends on the level of activity undertaken and the size and sex of the person concerned. A man 1.83m tall weighing 83kg uses a minimum of 80 calories per hour just to stay alive in a state of complete rest. The corresponding figure for a woman 1.52m tall weighing 45kg is 52 calories per hour. Athletic activity raises these figures considerably.

Energy requirements are met by the oxidation (burning) of food or stored energy within the body. The useful constituents of food and their calorie yields are as follows:

1 gramme of carbohydrate yields 4 calories
1 gramme of fat yields 9 calories
1 gramme of protein yields 4 calories
1 gramme of alcohol yields 7 calories

These figures take account of losses (most noticeable in the case of protein) within the body because of incomplete absorption.

Carbohydrates in food are the primary source of bodily heat and energy. They are digested by stages to produce glucose in, for the most part, the small intestine. From there glucose enters the bloodstream and is carried away to the muscles and liver where it is stored as glycogen. The muscles store 250 grammes or more of glucose in this form and the liver a further 100 grammes. Some glucose circulates in the blood (0.08 to 0.14 per cent) where it helps to maintain metabolism; low levels of blood glucose are associated with certain comatose conditions. An excess of glucose is converted with the aid of insulin to liver glycogen, but when the liver glycogen stores are full the surplus is converted to fat and stored in tissue beneath the skin. The amount of glycogen available to the body is a controlling factor in endurance, but it can be increased by dietary manipulation and training.

The voluntary muscles over which an athlete has direct control are bundles of long, thin fibres intertwined with blood vessels, nerves and quantities of fat. These fibres are bunched together at each end and attach to the skeleton across a mobile joint. A single fibre may be up to 40mm long; its sole function is to shorten (by up to 40 per cent) when mobility is required in the joint it serves. The fibres of voluntary muscle are criss-crossed internally with coiled filaments of protein. Chemical coupling and uncoupling of these filaments within a fibre creates the contraction and relaxation necessary to produce movement. An increase in tension not followed by movement is known as isometric contraction of the muscle fibres; when movement follows the contraction is described as isotonic.

The power developed by a muscle is proportional to the number of fibres it comprises. Recent research has identified two types of muscle fibre which are found in different proportions in different muscles: slower-working dark fibres and fast-contracting pale fibres. This suggests that the rate at which a muscle develops power, and consequently the rate of work necessary to train it further probably varies from muscle to muscle. The speed with which muscles can be activated depends on the length of the brain/muscle fibre link and on the delay in deciding what action to take. This stage of reaction can be shortened considerably in judo by familiarity with the patterns of judo movement. Repetition becomes experience which is stored as ready-processed patterns in the brain.

Muscle fibre is directly energized by the chemical breakdown of a compound called ATP (adenosine triphosphate). The productive breakdown of ATP depends on the efficiency with which glycogen can be broken down in tandem because the breakdown of glycogen (glycolysis) fuels the entire complex process. Glycolysis begins when the appropriate chemical messenger causes glycogen to revert to glucose. Thereafter a series of reactions occurs in two stages. At the end of the first stage glucose is reduced to pyruvic acid; if the heart and lungs are fit and efficient, sufficient oxygen is supplied to enable complete combustion of pyruvic acid which is thereby reduced to carbon dioxide and water. If, however, the heart-lung system is not fit enough, insufficient oxygen is supplied and the pyruvic acid already produced accumulates as lactic acid in the muscles. When the accumulation reaches intolerable levels the energy-giving process of glucose breakdown grinds to a standstill until such time as the lactic acid is dispersed.

As soon as lactic acid is produced there is a need for oxygen to assist in its dispersal: the heart-lung system owes oxygen. The body (particularly if trained) extends credit, but if the oxygen debt is not kept within the margin allowed the flow of energy dries up until the debt is brought under control. A joint effort by the heart-lung system (which by now is panting in an attempt to cope) and liver is required to reduce the debt; the former supplies the missing oxygen, the latter rebuilds lactic acid into glycogen.

Lactic acid is formed if the second stage of glucose break-down takes place in the absence of oxygen (i.e. anaerobically); a heart-lung system trained by exercise for efficiency supplies sufficient oxygen to enable the second stage of breakdown to take place in the presence of oxygen (i.e. aerobically). Fitness training prevents unnecessary oxygen indebtedness, although for reasons given in Chapter 29 a certain level of indebtedness is unavoidable in contest judo because oxygenation is physically restricted from time to time. The contest player should therefore use interval training to increase his margin of lactic acid tolerance.

CHAPTER 27. HEALTH

Fitness and health are separate concepts with deceptively little overlap. Clearly if health is used to describe freedom from disease it is possible to be healthy without being fit. Indeed it is possible to be fit for a sport such as boxing which actually contradicts the requirement of health in as much as it hurts the sportsman who plays it. That said, this chapter will spotlight a few aspects of health which have a bearing on judo practise.

Two matters of general concern are tobacco and alcohol. Smoking is a major public health issue and is impossible to defend except on the grounds of the pleasure it gives. There is ample evidence to suggest a positive link between smoking and bronchitis, arterial degeneration and lung cancer, and yet the public will not condemn what it sees as a private vice. Respect for privacy is one thing; athletic endeavour is another. Athletes who smoke (a smaller number do) know that smoking adds absolutely nothing to their performance. Moreover the habit is difficult to break and unpopular with non-smokers (i.e. most athletes). Non-smokers find the smell of stale tobacco which is dragged up from the lungs by hard judo practice quite unpleasant. From a purely physical point of view the habit is also worthless. The immediate effect of smoking a cigarette is startling: blood pressure rises and carbon monoxide (a poison) is introduced into the body. Carbon monoxide accounts for about 4 per cent of the smoke created; since it combines with about 250 times more haemoglobin (the means of transporting oxygen in the blood) than the same amount of oxygen, it is clearly monopolizing the blood transport system at the expense of valuable, life-giving oxygen. As a source of pleasure smoking is rotten value at the price.

Alcohol is also a socially-acceptable source of pleasure with a sting in its tail. It poses less of a threat to health than smoking, because in moderate quantities the body can metabolize alcohol before it does much harm. It is in fact both a drug and a sort of food. One gramme of alcohol yields seven calories of energy, which makes it a more concentrated source of energy than either protein or carbohydrates. The snag is that the release of energy is very slow (approximately forty-nine calories per hour), a fact which also prolongs the accompanying drug effect. As a sedative it depresses the central nervous system: motivation, concentration and co-ordination are impaired; blood pressure drops and temperature regulation is interfered with (sometimes for days on end); caution is over-ruled. Obviously it is unwise to drink during the final build-up to a contest. On the other hand, beer never tastes better than at the end of two hours' judo, so for those who enjoy a drink moderation is the golden rule.

Wine, women and song are the classic recipe for a decadent lifestyle. Wine has been dealt with and singing does no harm.

Sex, however, is still said by some people to milk an athlete of his vigour. That is not true. Neither intercourse nor masturbation have any direct effect on athletic performance. By the same token, abstinence does not store strength. Sex is a normal activity which does not conflict with training for a sport. The worst that can happen is that intensive training can lead to a loss of libido as a result of tiredness. The myth about sex during training was probably designed to avoid psychological complications concerning this type of transient impotence. In reality the problem is so unlikely as not to be worth a second thought.

A modern problem which does deserve a second thought is that of training while the body is suffering from infection. Influenza, glandular fever, venereal disease and tooth decay are all examples of infections which can render training harmful. Influenza is a scourge during the winter months and the widespread use of antibiotics has selectively developed increasingly virulent strains. Venereal disease and glandular fever are recognized as debilitating conditions and, as with influenza, training must be interrupted to allow a proper recovery. The same is true when tooth decay is allowed to go untreated; ultimately dental sepsis can destroy the valves of the heart in much the same way as rampant syphilis. There is one rule with no exception in sports training: that is *never train during or immediately after running a raised temperature because of infection*. The consequences could be fatal. In any event, steps should be taken to eliminate even minor infections because they devalue the effects of training.

Athlete's foot and verrucas are two afflictions which can make a judo player very unpopular if he goes on the mat with them untreated. They are both easily transmitted by treading where an infected foot has trod. Athlete's foot is a complaint in which the skin becomes inflamed, itchy and spongelike in appearance. A verruca is a form of wart which burrows into the horny layers of the skin, usually on the sole of the foot. The former can be treated with Whitfield's ointment made to order by a pharmacist or with mycil powder. A verruca requires conscientious treatment and dressing; often the wart can be removed by chemical action but in some cases it must be cut or burned out under medical supervision. Both infections persist in the footwear so care must be taken to avoid self re-infection.

Finally, since it is beneficial to see what an opponent is doing or what the scores are during contest, short-sighted players should consider wearing contact lenses for greater convenience on and off the mat. Hard plastic lenses are as cheap as fashionable spectacles and with persistence full tolerance to their presence in the eye can be built-up over two or three weeks. Soft porous lenses can be worn by anyone without acclimatization, but they are more expensive and have a shorter life span. Many sportsmen have found near-normal sightedness during activity a great blessing.

CHAPTER 28. DIET

Sportsmen as a class have always ritualized their diet. Despite folklore to the contrary, however, there is no need for that. The basic dietary ingredients are the same for everybody: proteins, fats, carbohydrates, mineral salts, vitamins and water. An athletic lifestyle only affects the quantities in which some of the ingredients are taken.

Proteins are exceedingly complex substances. They are constructed with some or all of twenty different amino acids; digestion of protein extracts the amino acids and releases them into the bloodstream. Given the right basic materials, the liver can manufacture all except eight of them; the eight which must be introduced via the diet are termed 'essential' amino acids. Once absorbed into the body they are carried in the blood plasma ready to meet the demands of cellular growth and repair; body proteins are created and renewed ceaselessly from the amino acids in this reservoir. It is worth knowing that all protein breaks down into useful material regardless of cost: steak, eggs and rice will provide the 'essentials'.

The value of protein food is set by the number of amino acids it contains. Egg white (albumen) contains all twenty and is used as a reference point. A league table of important protein sources in descending order of value is as follows:

(1) eggs
(2) milk
(3) beef
(4) soya beans
(5) rice
(6) wheat
(7) maize

Protein sources may be either animal or vegetable; animal sources generally provide better value on the amino acid scale than vegetable sources, but vegetarian athletes legitimately point out that many animals derive all their protein from vegetable sources and that man could do the same with a combination of vegetables in his diet.

Contrary to popular belief, protein cannot be stored in the body. Adequate protein is necessary to prevent the body from degrading its existing protein structures, but excess protein is soon neutralized by the increased elimination of nitrogen in urine. High-protein diets are a waste of money; the body takes what it needs (approx. 0.7gm per kg of body weight) from food and dispenses with the rest. Although cellular repair has first call on digested protein, energy needs can be met from the surplus once the nitrogen it contains has been removed. Four calories per gramme can be achieved following the removal of nitrogen as ammonia; ammonia, however, is poisonous and must rapidly be converted to urea and excreted by the kidneys in urine. Protein is inherently a secondary source of energy in diet.

Many foods contain protein; the following are listed in descending order of unit protein content:

(1) cheddar cheese
(2) sardines
(3) haddock
(4) beef
(5) poultry
(6) eggs
(7) barley
(8) peanuts
(9) lentils
(10) rice
(11) baked beans
(12) peas
(13) dried apricots
(14) milk
(15) potatoes
(16) bananas

Fats, including oils, are the richest heat-producing food. They have a higher calorific value than either protein or carbohydrates, but they are not favoured by the body as an independent source of energy. Too fast a breakdown of fat (as when insufficient or no carbohydrate is available) produces an accumulation of ketones toxic to the brain. Ketosis accounts for the illness which accompanies a crash diet to lose weight. Ideally the metabolism must maintain a balance between the rates of fat and carbohydrate breakdown; energy should be supplied predominantly by carbohydrate breakdown with some support from the fat reserves.

Fat consumed in food is emulsified in the duodenum to render it water soluble. Pending transfer to the fat depots, small droplets of oil can be detected in the blood stream for several hours following ingestion. No matter how urgent the body's need, fat is put into store before being mobilized as energy. Breakdown follows a similar pattern to that of glucose. Fat is initially reduced to glycerol and fatty acids, which, unless expended as energy, will recombine to form body fat again. In terms of calories, fat is a useful nutrient. It is obtained from animal and vegetable sources such as:

margarine
butter
bacon
beef
pork sausages
eggs
milk
cheese
herrings
olive oil
coconut

All carbohydrates in diet furnish the body with glucose for use as heat and energy. The metabolism of glucose has already been described (Chapter 26). Carbohydrates take the form of sugars and starches which, with the exception of milk, are derived from vegetable sources. Major carbohydrate foods in descending order of unit carbohydrate content are as follows:

(1) rice
(2) spaghetti
(3) honey
(4) oatmeal
(5) jam
(6) dates
(7) bread
(8) bananas
(9) potatoes

The mineral and vitamin content of a diet is as important as its energy content. Many, many minerals have been identified as playing a role in nutrition; most are only required in minute quantities and the surest way to obtain the quota is to eat a varied diet. The only conceivable deficiencies in a normal diet would concern iron and calcium, both of which can be guaranteed by the inclusion of milk, eggs, cheese, green vegetables, liver and sardines.

New vitamins are still being discovered and the true significance of those already known is also a matter for further research. The general understanding of vitamins is summarized below:

VITAMIN	FUNCTION	SOURCES
A	assists growth; maintains skin and cellular membrane	fish liver oils; dairy food; egg yolk; carrots
B complex (covers many types)	carbohydrate breakdown; protein metabolism; formation of blood and nerve fibres	yeast; wholemeal flour; liver; eggs; green vegetables
C	tissue and cell formation; bones; teeth	rose hip syrup; citrus fruits; green vegetables; new potatoes
D	enables calcium absorption	sunlight on skin; fish; eggs; dairy food
E	not known	wheat germ; milk; green vegetables
K	promotes proper blood clotting	green vegetables; soya beans

The cardinal rule is that vitamins must be obtained from fresh food; overcooking destroys them and they soon depart from lacklustre vegetables.

Water has no nutritive value, undergoes no chemical change in the body and yet is essential to life. It is more serious to be deprived of water than of any other item of diet, for without it the transport of nutrients is hampered, the cellular environment becomes increasingly hostile to life and the tissues are damaged by mineral imbalance. Never less than 65 per cent of body weight is water; an average-sized man will possess approximately 45 litres of which 70 per cent is contained within his cells, 23 per cent in the tissues and 7 per cent in plasma. The endless exchange of water between body fluids ensures that all is filtered through the kidneys about four times daily.

Fluid loss is a continuous process which since the body cannot store water like a camel, must be balanced by a corresponding intake. Water is lost through the skin as sweat and less perceptible 'seepage' and through the bodily orifices (continuously by expiration as water vapour and in urine, intermittently in vomit, diarrhoea or a streaming cold). The loss is made good by taking food and drink and by the biochemical release of water internally. Foods such as apples, potatoes and eggs have a high water content and significant amounts of water are obtained from solids in the diet. Thirst governs when, and how much, an athlete ought to drink. It is necessary for a competitor to avoid dehydration and this entails replenishment during the day, as well as some (to the limit of comfort) intake in anticipation; only a fool goes short of fluid willingly, for the consequences can cause severe bodily shock.

There is no wonder food for athletes. Milk is the next best thing in as much as it contributes to every class of nutrient; babies can live on it, although athletes have needs which it could not supply except in disproportionate quantities. One pint of milk can yield 380 calories of energy; it would not however be desirable to meet a requirement of 3000 calories by drinking eight pints of milk. The necessary variety would be missing and protein, carbohydrate and fat would be supplied in unsatisfactory proportions: athletes in training are advised to draw their calories in the form of one part protein to one part fat to four parts carbohydrate. For those who find milk palatable, a requirement of 1500 calories could be met by supplementing milk as follows:

1500 cals. requirement apportioned in the ratio			necessitates intake of	milk (1 pt) yields	supplement to be supplied
protein:	250 cals	1 part	62.5 gm	19 gm	43.5 gm
fat:	250 cals	1 part	27.8 gm	22 gm	5.8 gm
carbohydrate:	1000 cals	4 parts	250.0 gm	27 gm	223.0 gm

Rouge (France) executes *hanegoshi* from a neck and lapel grip. Note the drawing action of the right hand. Despite having his arm free the defender was unable to get his hand to the mat. Score: *ippon.*

The table indicates that one pint of milk should be supplemented by a largely fat-free diet in order to give 1500 calories in the right proportions; the margin of missing

carbohydrate over protein also gives scope for bulk and choice in the diet: cereals, rice and fruit would be a relatively cheap way of achieving the target figure.

Dietitians regularly estimate optimum calorie requirements, but without detailed observation no precise figure can be fixed for a sportsman in training. Every litre of oxygen taken up by the body exhausts, in due course, five calories of heat and energy. Inspired air contains 21 per cent

oxygen (approximately), expired air 16 per cent; oxygen uptake is therefore about 5 per cent by volume of throughput. In all cases the unknown quantity is the rate of respiration, which depends on variables like emotion, exertion and cardiac efficiency. The likely requirement of an active athlete is within the range 3500 to 4500 calories (male), 3000 to 4000 (female) per day of activity.

CHAPTER 29.   TRAINING FOR FITNESS

In judo the relationship between practice and fitness training is such that as skill increases it becomes necessary to develop fitness separately. Practice always contributes to skill, but when a player enjoys a margin of superiority over his opponent he can apply skill without having to be particularly fit. An absence of physical pressure causes a drop in the standard of fitness. This results in an inability to participate skil-fully in competition against equals with whom there is no freedom from exertion. Since progress depends on perform-ance against them, there must be specific preparation for the demands of competitive judo.

Undemanding practice uses as much time as hard judo against equals, but each tends

to lack the advantages of the other. Contest (real or simulated) is excellent preparation for contest. It is not, however, the most effective way of improving technical ability, and if relied on to make judo itself the source of fitness it is extremely arduous. Constructive mat work (for skill) backed up by systematic training (for fitness) strikes the right balance. It avoids the need for ever harder workouts with ever more experienced opponents and can develop essential characteristics faster than judo alone.

Training is an attempt to by-pass the ordinary timetable of development. An athlete analyses the characteristics which are the hallmark of a champion in his chosen sport. Rather than wait for cumulative

experience to endow him with those attributes he then devises methods for selectively enhancing those that are needed from among those he already possesses. Even though many immeasurable qualities go to make a champion, selective training methods are of proven effectiveness in respect of those capabilities which are quantifiable.

In order to devise effective training methods a sport is analysed in abstract terms, then in specific terms. Dr Ken Kingsbury, medical adviser to the BJA, has thoroughly examined the demands to be met by a judo player in contest. He found that judo is a whole body sport in which contest imposes a heavy burden on the upper body. The workload of competition requires stamina allied to a capacity for sudden explosive bursts of effort. Dynamic strength is necessary to throw an opponent, but maintenance of posture is associated with pronounced isometric activity in large groups of muscles. He also endorsed the view that the rapid changes of pace and direction featured in judo denote a high level of flexibility and agility.

One particular aspect of judo attracted Dr Kingsbury's attention: 'mat fitness'. When it comes to judo, very fit athletes from other sports are unable to go the pace without preparation for mat work. In conventional terms judo champions exhibit the same standard of fitness as champions in other spheres. They develop comparable degrees of efficiency in the

Photo 1—Response to attack Avoidance. Chochoshvilli (USSR) makes a breathtaking attack with *hizaguruma* against Uemura (Japan). Uemura with great presence of mind grasps the attacking leg with his right hand and slips his right knee clear.

heart-lung system, so enabling enough oxygen to reach the muscles in support of a high rate of glycogen breakdown, but the fact that even fit people find judo exhausting points to the conclusion that mat fitness goes beyond oxygenation. Dr Kingsbury identifies the missing ingredient as an ability to cope with the restricted oxygenation inherent in judo.

No matter how fit a judo player may be (and at the top they must be very fit indeed) the sport itself prevents full oxygenation of the muscles at times of effort. Rapid changes of pace and direction create a demand for oxygen which cannot be met instantaneously; moreover the oxygen supply system is likely to be inhibited anyway because the isometric contraction necessary to maintain posture compresses blood vessels within the muscles and because exertion in a fixed

Photo 2—The relentless attack carries thrower and defender upwards off the mat. Uemura levers his body away from a back-down position, thereby depriving the thrower of an *ippon*. Score: *waza-ari*.

Photo 1—Left-hand *haraigoshi* from a neck and mid-sleeve grip. The opponent has lost his right hand hold as a result of the thrower's left arm action. What threatens to become a sprawling fall . . .

Photo 2—. . . develops into a superb
ippon as the thrower bends at the knee
and steers his opponent directly
downwards with his chest.

chest position restricts breathing temporarily. At such times the energy demand must be met anaerobically; lactate levels rise (see Chapter 26) and if the levels reached are intolerable strength is sapped and skill is muted.

In the light of this analysis, the physical training objectives of a judo programme are:

(i) **to develop an efficient oxygen supply system (i.e. heart, lungs and muscles)**

(ii) **to develop a capacity for anaerobic activity**

(iii) **to develop dynamic and isometric strength**

These objectives must be achieved by methods which variously:

Exercises:
Bench Squats:

Stand upright on a gymnasium bench, feet together. Jump down, legs astride, and bend the knees so that the buttocks touch the bench. Immediately jump back up into the start position. Repeat until unable to continue.

Exercises: Prone Crawling:
Lie face down on the mat, arms stretched out in front with palms and forearms down. Raise the legs through 45° and keep them raised. Pull the body forward with clenched fists using only the arms. Race other players across the mat using either alternate or double arm action.

153

(1) work the whole body
(2) emphasize upper body involvement
(3) incorporate explosive bursts of effort
(4) require endurance
(5) are multidirectional
(6) develop agility and mobility.

The desired training objective is achieved by varying one or more of the following:

(a) the rate of movement
(b) the resistance encountered
(c) the duration of the activity
(d) the number of times an exercise is repeated

The first step in building a programme is to choose a number of exercises which between them cover all the criteria listed at (1)-(6) above. Some suggestions are:

skipping
rope climbing
running (forwards, backwards, on all fours)
swimming
weight training
uchikomi
squash
volleyball
press ups
prone crawling
squat thrusts
bunny hops

Exercises: Squat Thrusts:

Adopt a press-up position.
Bring the knees up to the elbows; immediately thrust back to the start position. Repeat; aim for speed against the clock.

Exercises: Cat Stretches:

Adopt a press-up position with the hands and legs further apart than usual.
Dip down and through between the arms, grazing the mat with nose, chin, chest and ribs in one continuous movement. Reverse the sequence. Repeat. Build up the number of repetitions.

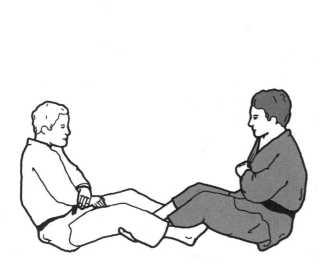

Exercises: Sit Ups:

Adopt a sitting position and link legs with another player. Place the hands behind the head or inside the collar at the neck. Sit up and lie back repeatedly while your partner holds your legs firm for leverage. Build up the number of repetitions.

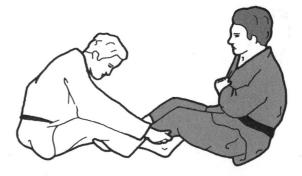

The second stage is to adjust one or more aspects (listed (a)-(d)) of the exercise in order to promote one or other of the objectives (i) to (iii) Take running as an example. Squad members use it to achieve objectives (i) and (ii). Distance running (say 3000m) repeated every other day at 60 to 70 per cent effort increases the efficiency of the heart and lungs (objective (i)). Shuttle running (sprinting backwards and forwards over a distance of 20m to 30m) for say 60 seconds, followed by 120 seconds of rest before repeating the exercise three or more times raises anaerobic capacity (objective (ii)). If light weights (1kg to 2kg) are carried there will also be an emphasis on upper body involvement (criterion (2) above). Interval training (work alternating with rest) can be used with most exercises to increase aerobic capacity or anaerobic capacity according to the length of work and rest periods. With rest periods twice as long as work periods, it has been found that exercise in ten second intervals trains an athlete to produce energy aerobically; thirty second work intervals create a significant demand for anaerobic energy after about ten minutes; sixty second intervals call for the anaerobic breakdown of glucose almost immediately.

Weight training and the use of devices such as the 'Bullworker' are most appropriate for achieving objective (iii). Isometric power is developed by maintaining exertion against high resistance; dynamic strength is increased by repeated exertion against lower resistances. On the principle that training must reflect the sport to be played, the resistances encountered by the weight-trainer must (a) be moved the way an opponent would be moved, (b) resist from the direction an opponent would resist from. Weight training which only overcomes gravity is not specific enough for judo.

Enough information has been given to enable a player to keep himself fit for judo. The range of activities relied on is a matter of taste but it is important to realize that fitness is the product of work. Only the person concerned knows how hard he is working: as a rough guide nothing less than 50 per cent effort is likely to have a significant effect on fitness unless repeatedly carried to the point of exhaustion, in which case endurance will be increased. Fifty to seventy per cent effort has a training effect; frequency determines whether the result is progression or maintenance. Above 70 per cent the effect is progressive and time available for training is the only real limitation on how much progress is made.

Time is a limiting factor in every programme. This has increased the popularity of circuit training as a comprehensive drill in which all the necessary criteria can be met. Nevertheless, exercise for its own sake can be tedious and judo players tend to prefer exercise with a competition element. Shuttle runs in the form of team races are convenient in this connection. The monotony of unadorned effort is avoided by a compact and beneficial exercise which is used to advantage by members of the different national squads in Great Britain.

The aim of this chapter is to present three specimen exercise programmes as alternative models for an imaginary two-hour mat session. Each programme serves a different objective: format A caters for coaching and for *kata* development; format B is a general programme with provision for formal instruction; format C is designed as a straightforward training programme. Every player should incorporate at least two different formats in his training schedule according to his degree of participation in the sport.

Training schedules are drawn up by reference to a convenient calendar period such as a fortnight or a month. A club player with no contest ambitions should reckon on eight hours judo a fortnight in order to maintain progress in the art. His schedule can usefully cover four two-hour sessions a fortnight, using the format pattern *A B A B*.

The contest man with limited time for training should aim for four or five two-hour sessions in the same period; four sessions will be beneficial with a format pattern of *A B C B*; the player who is looking for top honours must accommodate at least a mat session every other day. His fortnight's schedule will be arduous, something like *A B C B C B*.

Time spent on judo or judo skill training ought to be balanced by half as much time again (approximately) on systematic fitness training of the type described in Chapter 29. A comparison of the judo and non-judo times in the specimen formats reveals a built-in exercise debt for each. The non-judo time in the format is already given over to fitness training methods, but extra time must be spent on fitness training when the session has ended (and when convenient) if the balance referred to above is to be maintained; this extra time is identified as exercise indebtedness.

A player should satisfy both his on-the-mat and extra fitness requirements with a standard of exercise appropriate to his degree of involvement in the sport. Club level participation warrants general fitness; contest judo attaches a premium to endurance; championship judo calls for strength and endurance. Duly adjusted to the player's needs, shuttle running, circuit training or weight training can supply the desired effect.

Adjustment is carried out by reference to the principles contained in the previous chapter; the broad principle is that low repetition–high resistance exercises develop strength whereas high repetition–low resistance exercises develop endurance.

FORMAT A: COACHING/KATA DEVELOPMENT PROGRAMME

loosening-up exercises	10 minutes (non-judo time)
ancillary skill training	10 minutes
instruction	10 minutes
skill practice	35 minutes
instruction	25 minutes
skill practice	20 minutes
loosening-up exercises	10 minutes (non-judo time)
	Total 2 hours

NOTES:
(1) Ancillary skill training denotes such aspects as *uchikomi, ukemi, kata* (in a coaching programme) and crash mat practice.
(2) Periods allotted for instruction cover demonstration and practice by the class.
(3) Skill practice denotes judo itself either restricted (e.g. groundwork, left-handed throwing only, one attacking one defending, one blindfolded, specified throw only, armlocks only) or unrestricted *randori*.
(4) The ratio of judo to non-judo exercise creates an exercise debt of approximately fifteen minutes fitness training whenever this programme is used.

FORMAT B: GENERAL TRAINING PROGRAMME WITH INSTRUCTION

loosening-up exercises	10 minutes (non-judo time)
ancillary skill training	10 minutes
fitness training	10 minutes (non-judo time)
skill practice	35 minutes
instruction	25 minutes
skill practice	20 minutes
loosening-up exercises	10 minutes (non-judo time)
	Total 2 hours

NOTES:
(1) Ancillary skill training as for Format A.
(2) Fitness training denotes exercise of a quality appropriate to the players' standard of judo.
(3) Instruction time covers demonstration and practice by the class. The time allotted should vary according to the need for instruction: post-basic *kyu* grades a quarter of the available time; higher *kyu* grades one eighth of the available time. Advanced players using this programme should self-instruct and analyse technique. Any increase in instruction time should be at the expense of the first skill practice period; a decrease in instruction time should increase the second skill practice period.
(4) Skill practice as for Format A.
(5) The ratio of judo to non-judo exercise creates a negligible exercise debt of approximately three minutes for this programme.

FORMAT C: TRAINING EMPHASIS PROGRAMME

loosening-up exercises	10 minutes (non-judo time)
ancillary skill training	20 minutes
pressure training	25 minutes
skill practice	15 minutes
fitness training	15 minutes (non-judo time)
pressure training	25 minutes
loosening-up exercises	10 minutes (non-judo time)
	Total 2 hours

NOTES:
(1) Ancillary skill training as for Format A.
(2) Pressure training denotes hard non-stop judo either standing, on the ground or both; line-ups; contests, paced *uchikomi.*
(3) Skill practice as for Format A, but not too demanding (e.g. pre-arranged *randori,* throw for throw).
(4) Fitness training as for Format B.
(5) The ratio of judo to non-judo exercise creates an exercise debt of approximately eight minutes fitness training whenever this programme is used.

Relatively few injuries occur in judo given that it is a contact sport. Most of them are not particularly serious and nearly all of them could be avoided with care. The real cause of injury is often something other than judo itself. Lack of experience, for example, leads to knocks and abrasions among beginners; their natural clumsiness gets the better of them unless *dojo* discipline is strictly maintained. Likewise lack of fitness takes its toll in terms of sprains and muscular discomfort among players who insist on competing beyond their present level of fitness. Perhaps the most common cause of all is insufficient time spent loosening up before practice. Judo possesses a range of stretching exercises that is the envy of other sports; these should be performed religiously before practice so that pain can be saved for when it really is unavoidable.

Beginners inflict injury on themselves and other people because they do not relax sufficiently. Their movements are frantic. This results in such irritations as a sore nape of the neck because of indiscriminate jacket-pulling; stubbed toes as a result of anxious footwork; matburns on the feet and elbows because of incoherent twisting and turning; bruises on the ankles and shins because of badly-executed *ashiwaza*. Prevention is a relaxed approach to practice; cure for the consequences consists in keeping abrasions clean and antiseptic at all times: sticking plasters are rarely convenient during judo practice and a good alternative is a spray-on antiseptic coating from an aerosol. Stubbed toes can be temporarily bandaged to an adjacent toe. Soreness is alleviated by quality skin creams; arnica ointment is a herbal preparation useful for bruises.

The correct way to grip an opponent's jacket was described earlier. By not using the fingers and thumb as a vice, this grip saves injury. There is a risk with a finger and thumb grip that the thumb might get caught in the jacket with a painful consequence. Moreover, by curling wrist and fingers inwards on the hand at the opponent's lapel, a player avoids straining his wrist and forearm when throwing. Unless finger nails are kept short they can be torn off when an opponent defends by breaking away from an attack.

Analysis of the type and incidence of judo injuries has shown that sprains and tears account for the bulk of disability. Ankles and knees are most prone to injury followed by the shoulders, back and wrists. When fractures do occur they tend to concern the collar bone or ribs, both of which mend quite readily.

Knee injuries in particular are dreaded by contest men. The knee joint is not, in the western world, sufficiently flexible for the rigours of judo. Flexibility increases with practice, but there remains a chance that if a knee is rotated when bent and under load one of its semi-lunar cartilages (buffers of gristle) may split or dislocate. Embarrassingly the knee joint then develops a habit of locking straight and giving way unexpectedly with the result that the damaged cartilage must be removed by surgery. Removal does no harm but to get a player back on the mat after five weeks requires perseverance with knee exercises. Brian Jacks has had three cartilages removed at various times and still returned to Olympic competition. Humorists began to say that promotion above 3rd *dan* depended on the number of cartilages removed. Nevertheless a word of warning is required. Do not assume that every knee injury produces a torn cartilage. Strains and sprains of the supporting ligaments and muscles are far more common; they mimic the effects of cartilage damage but given time

will heal. The rule is surgery only when certain.

Injury to the shoulder is invariably the consequence of landing point down on one side, as when a thrower fails to turn his victim onto his back. The ligaments which bind the collar bone to the top of the shoulder blade are torn as the latter tries to thrust its way upwards on impact. The joint becomes tender and, depending on the severity of injury, may be dislocated so that a noticeable 'step' appears on the shoulder line. Too early a return to judo ensures that although the injury heals the step will remain. Positive efforts must be made at the outset to raise the shoulder and reduce the protuberance if such judo 'bumps' are to be avoided.

Self-medication is only advisable in the case of plain and straightforward injuries, the type of injuries for which a doctor would prescribe the very treatment described below. In other cases injured persons must use their common sense and consult a doctor as necessary. Never take chances.

Experience has shown that the pain and swelling associated with sprains and tears can be counteracted by immediate cold treatment. Heat and massage are not appropriate at that stage. As soon as possible cold treatment should be applied to the site of the injury. This can be done with ice from a vacuum flask, with cold storage packs such as are used to keep picnic baskets cool or with a towel soaked in cold water. The bodyweight should be kept off the injury. It is useful to apply pressure (except where fractures are known or suspected to have occurred) in the form of a padded elastic bandage in order to reduce swelling. Cold treatment is then repeated at intervals until the prospect of further swelling has abated. The early reintroduction of movement (within the limits of pain) is very helpful for proper rehabilitation; unnecessary immobility is, in fact, counterproductive.

Judo players as a breed usually struggle back on to the mat if at all possible when there is something at stake. Some of them even manage to win championships with broken ribs and sprained backs, but medically speaking the practice is ill-advised. Strapping and anaesthetising aerosols can never take the place of rest and proper management; in time the body will react by taking three weeks to clear up injuries that used to vanish in one. When that happens an enforced break from judo may be necessary to regain health. Proper management consists in gradually bringing the injured area back into full use, always within the limits of pain. The return to mat work may warrant the use of support bandages initially. Rubber inner tubes cut in strips of the right length and width are ideal: they stretch and can be fastened by tucking the end under the support section. However, no form of bandage should be used longer than necessary. To do so invites dependence on the artificial support and the joint becomes unsatisfactorily weak as its muscles begin to waste.

Very occasionally someone manages to hit their head on the mat during practice. Concussion may follow even though there has been no loss of consciousness; the symptoms include nausea, headache, drowsiness, confusion, impaired vision or slurred speech according to severity. The proper course of action is to rest and cease all activity until well again. Never carry on with the activity; never take any alcohol during the aftermath. Concussion often permits a lucid interval which gives way to the effects of impact some time later. A concussed person should be carefully observed with this in mind. If there has been a loss of consciousness the person concerned should be taken to the casualty department of a hospital.

Sports injuries enjoy a mixed reception from the medical profession. In some quarters they are seen as self-inflicted wounds suffered by people in a hurry to get back and do the same again. Elsewhere sympathetic doctors try to speed the return to active sport.

In a search for effective remedial treatment (particularly in the case of back injuries) sportsmen quite commonly turn to osteopaths and physiotherapists for help. No hard and fast rule governs where the best treatment is to be found. Dr Kingsbury's personal opinion is that:

'It seems safe and fair to say, however, that at present, and in general, my experience over the last four to five years would lead me to go to an osteopath first if I had a stiff aching back or some restricted joint or spinal movement and I felt quite normal otherwise, whereas I would go to a physiotherapist for a muscular-ligament injury of the back or elsewhere; and seek a medical opinion if I felt otherwise unwell. In any case, I would seek further medical opinion where the pain was severe, if the symptoms continued or the treatment did not seem completely to cure the condition.

This opinion is personal and readers must make up their own minds on where best to seek treatment for judo injuries.

Notes

The following glossary includes most of the Japanese terminology which is in common use in judo. It is not intended to be a fully-comprehensive dictionary of Japanese terms, only a guide to cover most judo circumstances. Generally, the names of techniques are derived from verbs, which when changed into a noun undergo certain superficial changes. In the glossary, therefore, the noun form is given, and then in brackets, the verb form (which can be looked up in a dictionary), for example – *harai (v. Harau)* – to sweep.

Where a noun is shown to have several numbered sub-divisions (e.g. kata) each sub-division has its own different Japanese ideograph. Reading it in Japanese would present no confusion but when the sound only is represented in English (phonetic) script, confusion can arise. The judo enthusiast should remember at all times that the English translation can only be, and is, *phonetic*. Some of the words included in this glossary are used solely in contests.

One might ask why judo retains the terminology of its origin – Japanese. As with music and fencing, it is found more convenient to maintain the original. It can be used as a *lingua franca* throughout the world which makes for convenience and efficiency in international relations. Japanese is fairly easy to pronounce. There is hardly any flexion and the voice pitch can be kept constant. The following grammatical rules may assist

with pronunciation, but like all grammatical rules they are often broken. However, they should prove sufficient for judo.
1. All consonants are hard, e.g. 'k' as in king.
2. Vowels must be pure, e.g. 'a' as in bat; 'e' as in set; 'i' as in bit; 'o' as in got.
3. Syllables for ease of pronunciation can be considered to consist of two letters generally, e.g. ka-ta-me-wa-za; tsu-ri-ko-mi-go-shi. The exceptions to this general rule are the five vowels and 'shi', 'tsu' and 'chi'. Each syllable should have equal stress.

Practice slowly and emphatically for some time; the terms will soon become easier, quicker and begin to sound more natural.

Selected common peculiarities
(a) If there are two consonants together each must be clearly pronounced, e.g. ippon – each 'p' clearly pronounced as in 'top pot'.
(b) It is common in Japanese for the consonants 'k', 't', 's' and 'h' to become hard when they appear in the middle of a word or combination of words. This is referred to by the Japanese as 'nigori'. Therefore 'k' becomes 'g', 't' becomes 'd', 'sh' becomes 'j' and 'h' becomes 'b', e.g. 'koshi' in koshiwaza becomes 'goshi' in haraigoshi. 'H' can be hardened a second time to become 'p', e.g. hon = a point, becomes ippon = one point.
(c) 'N' is the only consonant in Japanese not accompanied by a vowel. It should however be pronounced just as distinctly as if it were a couplet, e.g. ip-po-n-se-oi-na-ge.

Glossary

AIKI—A form of self-defence, based on special principles (*lit.* harmony of spirit).

AIKIDO—The 'way' of Aiki.

AITE—Opponent, partner.

ARASHI—Storm (e.g. yama arashi = mountain storm).

ASHI—Leg, foot.

ASHIWAZA—Leg/foot technique.

ATAMA—Head.

ATE—Strike, hit.

ATEMIWAZA—Hitting or punching technique.

AYUMI ASHI—A manner of walking in which each foot leads the other successively.

BUDO—Military arts/concepts.

BUJITSU—Martial arts (all inclusive).

BUSHI—A knight of feudal Japan (a social class).

BUSHIDO—The moral ethical code of the Bushi, formulated originally *c.* 14th century.

BUTSUKARI—See UCHIKOMI.

CHITSAI—Small.

CHIKARA—Strength.

CHUI—A caution (penalty; equivalent to 5 points).

DAN—'Leader' grade, generally black belt.

DE—(v. DERU)—To come out, to advance. (e.g. deashiharai).

DO—(a) Way, path, etc. This word was used frequently in Chinese and Japanese philosophy in the sense of the way of doing an act in the moral and ethical sphere as well as the simple physical. Professor Kano 'borrowed' it from these sources.
(b) Trunk of the body.

DOJO—Hall or room in which judo is practised.

ERI—Collar, of a jacket.

FUSEGIKATA—Method, form, of defending.

FUSEGU—To defend.

GAKE (v. KAKERU)—To hang, hook, block.

GARAMI (v. GARAMU)—To entangle, wrap, bend.
GENKI—Energetic, lively, active.
GONOKATA—Forms of strength.
GOSHINJITSU—The art of self-protection (in all its forms).
GYAKU—Reverse, upside down.
HA—Wing.
HADAKA—Naked.
HAIRIKATA—The way of entering for a (technique).
HAJIME—Start, referee's call to commence a contest.
HANE—Spring (e.g. hanegoshi = spring hip).
HANSOKU—Disqualification (penalty; equivalent to ten points).
HANTAI—To oppose.
HANTEI—Judgement, the referee's call at the end of a drawn contest calling on the corner judges to indicate who in their opinion was the better of the two contestants.

HARA—Stomach.
HARAI (BARAI) (v. HARU)—Sweep, reap.
HIDARI—Left.
HIJI—Elbow.
HIKI (v. HIKU)—Pull.
HISHIGE (v. HISHIGU)—To crush, squash, smash.
HIZA—Knee.
HON—(a) Point (see IPPON); ultimate score awarded in a contest.
(b) Basic.
(c) Number suffix for counting long cylindrical objects, therefore ippon seoinage = one arm shoulder throw.
IPPON—One point (score value of ten points).
IPPON SOGO GACHI—Compound win by IPPON made up of a score of WAZA-ARI added to the benefit of a KEIKOKU penalty.

ITSUTSUNOKATA—Forms of five.
JI—A Japanese ideograph.
JIGOTAI—Defensive posture.
JIKAN—Time out (the referee's instruction to the timekeeper when a break or pause in the contest is necessary).
JITA KYOYEI—The principle that individual advancement benefits society as a whole.
JITSU (JIUTSU or JUTSU)—Art.
JOSEKI—The place in a dojo or hall where the seniors or VIPs sit.
JU—(a) Soft, gentle. This word is a word taken from Taoist philosophy and embodies the opposite of hard, extreme, unreasonable. Hence the use of ju in judo does not imply soft (as a synonym of easy), but rather reasonable, efficient. Physical action in judo is not meant to be easy (weak) so much as

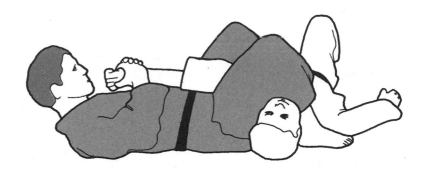

economic, by using the body to its best advantage and taking active advantage of any and all weaknesses the opponent may offer, so that maximum effect can be attained with maximum efficiency.
(b) Ten.
JUDO—A form of wrestling in which clothes are worn by the contestants. The clothes and belt (encircling the waist twice) allow for greater range of technique. The depth of judo in the use of **TACHIWAZA** (techniques done in the standing position) and **NEWAZA** (techniques done in groundwork positions) requires skill plus physical and mental fitness being increasingly raised to an extremely high standard. In promotion examinations (grading contests) no allowance

is conceded to size or weight; success depends solely on the individual's attributes.
JUDOGI—The clothes worn when practising or competing at judo.
JUDOKA—A person who practises judo. A very senior player (at least 4th dan).
JU-JUTSU (JIUJITSU)–A name covering all forms of fighting, without weapons, with very drastic methods.
JUNOKATA—The forms of 'gentleness'. Showing the principles of 'giving way'.
JUSHIN—Centre of gravity.
KAESHI (GAESHI)—To counter (e.g. osotogaeshi = major outer counter).
KAESHIWAZA—Counter techniques.
KAKE—The point of the throw, the point of maximum power.
KAI (KWAI)—Society, club.

KAKU (GAKU)—An angle.
KAMI—(a) Upper, top.
(b) Paper.
(c) God(s).
KAMIZA—'Upper seat'; the instructors' side of the DOJO.
KANSETSU—A joint, articulation.
KANSETSUWAZA—Technique of locking limb joints.
KAO—Face.
KARATE—(Literally empty-handed) a system of fighting without weapons, striking with the hand, feet, elbows, etc.
KARATEDO—The 'way' of karate.
KARUI—Light.
KATA—(a) Form. A stylized set of techniques used to develop the performer's posture, balance and appreciation of the various judo techniques.
(b) One side.
(c) Shoulder (e.g. kataguruma = shoulder wheel).

   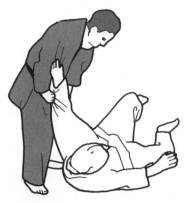

KATAI—Hard.
KATAME (GATAME) (v. KATEMERU)—To harden, tighten, hold (e.g. katagatame = shoulder hold).
KATSU (or KAPPO)—Methods of resuscitation.
KEIKO—Practise.
KEIKOKU—Warning (penalty; equivalent to 7 points).
KEMPO—A method of fighting, similar to boxing.
KEN—Sword.
KENDO—The 'way' of the sword (Japanese two-handed fencing).
KENDOGU—General equipment for practising kendo.
KERU—To kick.
KESA—A Buddhist monk's surplice, worn diagonally across the body. Thus there is the technique known as kesagatame but which in free translation into English is referred to as scarf hold.

KI—Psychic energy said to be centred in the SAIKATANDEN.
KIAI—A shout used to harden the body and strengthen the will when maximum effort is required.
KIME (v. KAKERU)—To decide.
KIMENOKATA—Forms of decision, which is the kata of self-protection.
KIRI (v. KIRU)—Cut, as with a knife.
KO—(a) small, minor (e.g. kouchigari = minor inner reaping).
(b) Old, ancient.
(c) Lecture, study, think.
KODOKAN—The headquarters of judo in Japan (Tokyo).
KOKA—A score, almost a yuko (value of score; 3 points).
KOSHI (GOSHI)—Hips, (e.g. koshiwaza = hip techniques).
KOSHIKINOKATA—The forms of the old style. All techniques are supposed to be performed in armour.

KUBI—Neck.
KUMIKATA—Method of holding the judogi.
KURUMA (GURUMA)—(a) Wheel (e.g. oguruma = major wheel). (b) Vehicle.
KUZURE (v. KUZURERU)—To crumble, collapse, break-down. Thus a free translation of kuzurekesagatame would be broken scarf hold.
KUZUSHI—The balance broken.
KYU—A judo 'student' grade.
MA—Exact, just, absolutely.
MACHI-DOJO—Back-street gymnasium.
MAE—Front.
MAKIKOMI—To wrap or roll up, to throw by rolling oneself so that the opponent is whipped off his feet.
MANAKA—Centre.
MASUTEMIWAZA—Technique whereby the performer (tori) falls straight on to his back.

MATA—The inside top of the thigh.
MATTE—Wait, break.
MAWARI (v. MAWARU)—To turn round.
MEIJIN—Expert, master.
MI—Body (human).
MIGI—Right (as opposed to left).
MIZU—Water.
MOMO—Thigh.
MON—Gate, junior grade.
MOROTE—Both hands, two hands (e.g. morote seoinage = both hands shoulder throw).
MUNE—Chest.
NAGE (v. NAGERU)—To throw (e.g. nage waza = throwing techniques).
NAGENOKATA—The forms of throwing. 15 selected throws executed both left and right to train the participants in body control and appreciation of judo technique.
NAME—Wave (of water).

NAMI (v. NARUBERU)—To place in a line, range in a row.
NE (v. NERU)—To lie down.
NEWAZA—Technique done in a lying down position.
O—Big, large, major (e.g. ouchigari = major inner reaping).
OBI—Belt.
OKII—Big.
OKURI (v. OKURU)—To send forward (e.g. okurierijime = sliding lapel neck-lock).
OSAEKOMI—Holding (e.g. osaekomiwaza = holding technique(s)); referee's call signalling to the time-keeper that a hold is effective.
OSHI (v. OSU)—To push.
OTOSHI (v. OTOSU)—To drop (e.g. taiotoshi = body drop).
OWARI—The end.
RANDORI—Free practice.
REI—Bow.
RENRAKU—Connection, contact.

RENRAKUWAZA—Combination technique.
RENSHU—To practise.
RENZOKUWAZA—Comprehensive name for throws linked up in any way.
RITSUREI—Standing bow.
RONIN-An unretained SAMURAI warrior.
RYOTE—Two hands.
RYU—School. Attached to most of the names of the old jiujitsu systems (e.g. Kito Ryu).
SAIKATANDEN—The lower abdomen.
SAMURAI—A knight of feudal Japan (a social class). (See bushi).
SASAI—To support, prop (e.g. sasaitsurikomiashi = propping drawing ankle).
SEI RYOKU SENYO—The principle of maximum efficiency in the use of mind and body.
SENAKA—The back (of a body).
SENSEI—Teacher, senior.

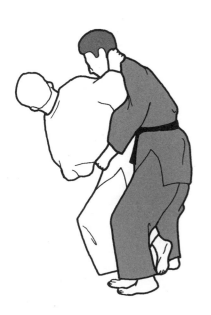

SENSHU—A competitor, champion.
SEOI (v. SEOU)–To carry on the back (e.g. seoinage).
SEPPUKU—The bushi method of committing suicide. Normally erroneously called 'harakiri'.
SHIAI—Contest.
SHIAIJO—Contest area.
SHIDO—Note (penalty; equivalent to 3 points).
SHIHAN—Master, past-master, founder.
SHIHO—Four quarters, four directions.
SHIKI—Style, ceremony.
SHIME (JIME) (v. SHIMERU)—To tighten, strangle.
SHIMEWAZA—Technique of neck-locking.
SHIMOZA—'Lower seat'; the ordinary members' side of the DOJO.

SHISEI—Posture.
SHITA—Below, underneath.
SHIZEN—Nature.
SHIZENTAI—Natural (upright) posture.
SODE—Sleeve.
SONOMAMA—Freeze, do not move.
SORE MADE—Referee's command: that is all, finish.
SOTO—Outside, outer (e.g. osotogari = major outer reap).
SUKUI (v. SUKUKU)—To scoop up.
SUMI—Corner.
SUTEMI (v. SUTERU)—To throw away.
SUTEMIWAZA—Technique whereby the attacker throws away his own body, sacrifices his own posture.
TACHI (v. TATSU)—To stand.

TACHIWAZA—Technique done in the standing position.
TAI—Body.
TAI-SABAKI—Body movement.
TAISO—Physical exercise.
TANI—Valley (e.g. taniotoshi = valley drop).
TATAMI—Rice straw mats used in dojos and Japanese houses.
TATE—Vertical.
TE—Hand (e.g. tewaza = hand techniques).
TEKUBI—Wrist.
TOKETA—Hold broken. A command given by a referee to indicate to the timekeeper, the contestants and the onlookers generally that a contestant has effectively broken the hold by which he was being secured.
TOKUI—Favourite, special (e.g. tokuiwaza = favourite technique).

TOMOE—Turning over, twisting over, whirling over. It is difficult to find the exact translation in English but tomoenage freely translated is commonly known in English as – stomach throw.

TORI (v. TORU)—(a) The name used often in technical explanation for the person who throws.
(b) To grasp, to hold in the hands.

TSUGI ASHI—A manner of walking in which one foot leads at each step and the other never passes it.

TSUKURI—The action of breaking the opponent's balance.

TSURI—To 'fish' up (e.g. tsurikomi = to 'fish', lift up and pull forward).

TSUYOI—Strong.

UCHIKOMI (v. UTSU)—To beat against. A repetitive exercise where the throwing technique is taken to the point of kake.

UDE—Arm.

UE—Above, on top of.

UKE (v. UKERU)—To take. The name used often in technical explanations for the person who is thrown.

UKEMI—The 'breakfall'.

UKI (v. UKU)—To float. Buoyant.

URA—Back, rear, reverse.

USHIRO—Behind, back of (e.g. ushirogoshi = back of hip).

UTSURI (v. UTSURU)—To change, move (e.g. utsurigoshi = changing hip).

WAKARE (v. WAKARU)—To divide, separate (e.g. yokowakare = side separation).

WAZA—Technique.

WAZA-ARI—A score, almost an ippon (score value of 7 points).

WAZA-ARI AWASETE IPPON—IPPON achieved by having scored two WAZA-ARIS.

YAMA—Mountain.

YOKO—Side (e.g. yokosutemiwaza – a sacrifice throw with the attacker falling onto his side in order to execute the technique).

YOSHI—Carry on. A referee's instruction to contestant to carry on with the contest.

YOWAI—Weak.

YUBI—Finger or toe.

YUKO—A score, almost waza-ari (score value of 5 points).

YUSEIGACHI—A win by superiority.

ZAREI—Kneeling bow.

ZAZEN—Sitting meditation.

ZORI—Toe grip straw sandals.

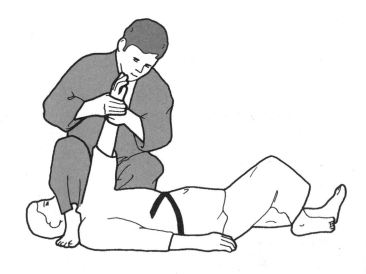

This list comprises the Gokyo plus the extra throws included in this book, and the groundwork techniques, titled in Japanese and English; the third column indicates the page on which the technique is analysed.

Gokyononagawaza—40 throwing techniques

Section 1—Daiikkyo

Deashiharai	Foot sweep throw	62
Hizaguruma	Knee wheel throw	59
Sasaetsurikomiashi	Propping drawing ankle throw	60
Ukigoshi	Floating hip throw	50
Osotogari	Major outer reap throw	58
Ogoshi	Major hip throw	46
Ouchigari	Major inner reap throw	57
Seoinage (morote)	Shoulder throw	40

Section 2—Dainikyo

Kosotogari	Minor outside reap throw	67
Kouchigari	Minor inner reap throw	63
Koshiguruma	Loin wheel throw	48
Tsurikomigoshi	Lift pull hip throw	51
Okuriashiharai	Side sweeping ankle throw	72
Taiotoshi	Body drop throw	39
Haraigoshi	Sweeping loin throw	49
Uchimata	Inner thigh throw	64

Section 3—Daisankyo

Kosotogake	Minor outside hook throw	69
Tsurigoshi	Lifting hip throw	47
Yoko-otoshi	Side drop throw	75
Ashiguruma	Leg wheel throw	71
Hanegoshi	Spring hip throw	53
Haraitsurikomiashi	Sweeping drawing ankle throw	61
Tomoenage	Stomach throw	77
Kataguruma	Shoulder wheel throw	42

Section 4—Daiyonkyo

Sumigaeshi	Corner throw	78
Taniotoshi	Valley drop throw	79
Hanemakikomi	Winding spring hip throw	54
Sukuinage	Scooping throw	84
Utsurigoshi	Changing hip throw	56
Oguruma	Major wheel throw	70
Sotomakikomi	Outer winding throw	45
Ukiotoshi	Floating drop throw	43

  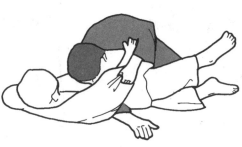

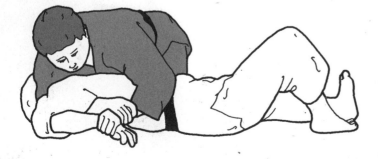